Stewart's poetry is born from his compassionate awareness. Every poem is an invitation to pay attention to what's going on in our world—and then we experience our own questions, insights, and wonder. We too wake up.

—Margaret Wheatley, author of many books,
Founder Warriors for the Human Spirit

Stewart Levine's poetry is playful, thoughtful, generous and kind. Through intimate poetic moments dedicated to one subject, Levine focuses his readers on one idea and offers inspiration and a space to contemplate and connect to our bigger selves. Stewart's poems are little gifts of insight and support as we journey through our days and our lives looking for a deeper connection to Source.

—Jennifer Abrams, MA, communications consultant and author of
Stretching Your Learning Edges: Growing (Up) at Work.

Stewart Levine's poetry is like stepping into an exotic land with its own rhythm, movement, and beauty. As a meditation, it can take you deeper into your own inner regions, revealing layers of meaning and consequence that nourish the soul.

—Alan Briskin, Ph.D, author, *The Stirring of Soul in the Workplace* and
co-author, *Daily Miracles.*

There is a succinct summary of profound truth found in the simple verse such as "peace is left after release, " "In discomfort hearts grow wise," "warring factions strangely serene." Stewart is downloading a cosmos "of divine-speak." Thank you for sharing your joy of creativity with my soul.

—Michele Jurika, MA, Coach and Therapist

Stewart Levine is a brilliant poet who captures the energy, ambiguity, depth, spirit and wit of the moment through his verses. I always can't wait to get Stewart's latest poems in my inbox. I am excited for them to finally be part of a book. Every thoughtful person should check out these poems and be prepared to be profoundly moved.

—Henry Yampolsky, J.D. mediator and best selling author
Dis-Solving Conflict from Within: An Inner Path for Conflict Transformation

Stewart's poetry always opens my mind up to new possibilities! He combines intellectual brilliance with human insights, and helps my heart glimpse a world that otherwise would be invisible to me.

—Kimberly Wiefling, Author of *Scrappy Project Management,*
Cofounder of *Silicon Valley Alliances*

The deeply engrained rhyming scheme in this poetry lulls the reader into a sort of reverie. There is much insight within the waves.

—Mícheál Ó Súilleabháin, Poet, Singer, and Speaker,
Author of ***Early Music*** published on Many Rivers Press

Stewart Levine's timely and thoughtful poems offer us both solace and a new way to view our world as it is right now. The prompts at the end of each poem stimulate deeper contemplation and exploration. A wonderful addition to the seeker's library.

—Perry Pidgeon Hooks, Founder , Hooks Book Events

Like fine wine Stewart's poems gently layer complexity with notes from the vines of our time. Some poems that get better with age, others that are most poignant when consumed upon receipt. Grab a glass and indulge in his shared verse.

—Anita Bahe, Ph.D., Environmental Activist

How many lawyers do you know who have the soul of a poet? Stewart Levine is an exemplar whose poetry is provocative yet lyrical, unflinching yet beautiful, inspiring and just plain enjoyable.

—Marilee Adams, Ph.D. Bestselling author of *Change Your Questions, Change Your Life: 12 Powerful Tools for Leadership, Coaching and Results*

Stewart's poetry shows a great understanding of humanity, our successes and our challenges. It is both beautiful and intellectual. It makes us think and gives us pause. A poem by Stewart makes every day a better day.

—Kathye Citron, Business Consultant

I marveled at how quickly and easily Stewart captured the essence of a thought in so few words. The depth and sensitivity to the human condition takes us to a new level of how to live life. The meanings are deep, coming from an innate storehouse of knowing and experience. The body of work is rich with variety, yet all based in how we humans conduct life. Stewart is someone I would consult as a sage or an "old soul" that offers much wisdom. As a daily reading people will benefit greatly. I can imagine readers buying copies as gifts delivering timeless messages...there is no end to the book's life!

—Peter Grazier, author, *Go Team! Take Your Team to the Next Level* (with Ken Blanchard), *Before It's Too Late*; *Power Up for Team Results Series*

Beautiful prose and insights from a pure heart. There is something magical about Stewart's poetry and what a treasure it is to have it in one place. What is fantastic is that it meets each of us where we are at this very moment. Stewart capture's life in poetic rhythm and at the same time, open us up to possibilities. From Doubt to Soaring and Serenity and Bliss, the poems open us to our great opportunities to live a healthy life. Reading this book is a gently transformational and healing experience.

—Ayelet Baron, Strategic Futurist and Multi-Award Winning Indie Author

STEWART LEVINE

PILGRIM'S PATH

Morning Practice for Seekers

The depth and mystery of God leaves all of us as perpetual searchers and seekers, always novices and beginners. It is the narrow and dark way of faith.

—RICHARD ROHR

Being a Pilgrim

To journey without being changed
is to be a nomad.
To change without journeying
is to be a chameleon.
To journey and to be transformed
by the journey is to be a pilgrim.

We all start out as pilgrims, wanting to journey and hoping to be transformed by the journey. But, just as it is impossible when listening to an orchestra to hear the whole of the symphony for very long before we are drawn to hear only the piano or the violin, in just this way, our attention to life slips and we experience people and places without being affected by their wholeness. And sometimes, feeling isolated and unsure, we change or hide what lives within in order to please or avoid others.

The value of this insight is not to use it to judge or berate ourselves, but to help one another see that integrity is an unending process of letting our inner experience and our outer experience completes each other, in spite of our very human lapses.

I understand these things so well, because I violate them so often. Yet I, as you, consider myself a pilgrim of the deepest kind, journeying beyond any one creed or tradition, into the compelling, recurring space in which we know the moment and are changed by it. Mysteriously, as elusive as it is, this moment-where the eye is what it sees, where the heart is what it feels-this moment shows us that what is real is sacred.

Mark Nepo
The Book of Awakening

ALSO BY STEWART LEVINE

Getting to Resolution: Turning Conflict Into Collaboration

The Book of Agreement: Getting the Results You Want

Collaboration 2.0: Best Practices for a Web 2.0 World (co-author)

The Best Lawyer You Can Be: Physical, Emotional, Mental and Spiritual Wellness (curator and editor)

For my Teachers and Mentors, too numerous to mention!

CONTENTS

March

April

May

June

July

August

September

October

November

December

Introduction

For many years it was my practice to make journal entries as a way to start the day, usually about one page of long hand automatic writing. In the fall of 2000 I was at a retreat on Whidbey Island in Washington State when my first poem emerged, twenty lines of iambic pentameter rhyme. Over the next three years I continued to produce poems. I would write down a one-word title and out would come about twenty lines of rhyme. I must admit to feeling more of a transcriber / curator / steward than a poet.

Between 2003 and 2010 I produced an occasional poem but also developed the facility for creating these rhymes on demand for special occasions. I was also told that before written history wisdom was passed along orally in the kind of verse I was producing. Around 2010 I had the journals digitized and edited by a poetry professor who was very encouraging. Over the past few years I have been polishing, adding reflective questions and attributing poems to calendar days.

It has been an awesome process! For many years I would enjoy the daily prose of Mark Nepo from "The Book of Awakening." A few years ago I decided it was "time to begin eating my own dog food!" So every day I begin with a careful reading of my own poem for the day. Most days I say "WOW!"

I hope you enjoy them half as much as I enjoyed putting together this anthology. I can promise that if you faithfully engage in the daily practice of reading and reflection for a year your life will be impacted. I look forward to learning about your experience.

Stewart Levine
December 15, 2022
Alameda, CA

January

1 FOCUS

Time to express what you think
No hiding behind eyes that blink
Laser intensity your clarity shines
Honor your thoughts and Divine's

No gibberish now or menacing fear
Your power the voice in your ear
Let many hear what you know
They honor wisdom thanking you so

Stay clear on your missions' plan
Manifest vision quick as you can
Not about the small ego you hold
About humanity your license bold

Mind weakness dragging your skirt
Don't be afraid of fingernail dirt
Attend wobble or babble within
Stalwart steadfast with a strong chin

Let go of shame and foolish pride
Chariot is fast on your noble ride
Clouds of illusion empty fake rain
Uncover resolve let go of false pain

Do you know the observer you see and can share something unique?
Are you developing, refining and communicating messages you came to deliver

2 COMPASSION

What quality do we all long for
Caring for others no matter what for
Knowing them better our close friends
Without agendas or hidden ends

A great source of pleasure and joy
Knowing each other be they girl or boy
Seeing their footsteps honoring their dreams
Helping achievement no matter what seems

Taking the time to connect at source
To honor their life with presence of course
Each of us wants to be known and seen
That we're not singular in pursuit of a dream

For those climbing steep hills all alone
To know they've got people rooting from home
The journey's not easy sometimes it gets tough
We need our cheerleaders when going is rough

Often on travels we see less fortunate one's
They clearly need help be they daughters of sons
Seeing folks clearly and their unique need
Provides opportunity to do a good deed

When out and about take time as you roam
See what is needed by others at the bone
What can you give and hwow can you serve
To cushion the jolts of lives at the verge

How can you honor the deep needs of others
How do you cherish and let go your druthers
Remember the joy giving gives back
Honor their void and shift your tack

Know you will find a great sense of yes
The smile in your mind from helping I guess
For in the end please do remember
The one who cared you'll be seen as tender

Can you take the time to scan for needs within the communities you inhabit?
What do you think you might receive in return for giving with compassion?

3 ALIGNMENT

Sense of balance pure equanimity
Internal congruence state of prosperity
Heart body mind entrained
Synchronicity of cells rearranged

Feeling of purpose on top of the world
Power turned on without any swirl
Internal voices quiet they purr
Sense of elation you're who you were

How lovely if the world were in tune
A bright summer day early in June
Floral fragrance sky diamond bright
Stars all aglow moon lighting night

One step another your vision bold
Imagine coherence with all in your fold
Friends family your team and clan
Town you live in each woman and man

Whatever was clouding heart mind
You have the tools to leave behind
When you're coherent aligned where you are
You can go anywhere real quick real far

*Do you feel a sense of alignment with those close to you, your community
and surroundings?*
What is out of alignment that needs a shared vision?

4 ENVISIONING

Most not sure what to do
React with haste sit and stew
Never bedrock or clear
No thinking about what is dear

Pointed focus with great strength
Indecision jaw is clenched
With misgivings uncertainty
Can't see a way to set you free

Find freedom avoid remorse
See consequence of a course
Planetary pain makes you scream
Unfiltered action without a dream

See yourself in every scene
Embody results live that dream
Get into feelings and mental sets
See it all before taking steps

Listen to voices from inside
Truthful beyond personal pride
Resist win/lose use common sense
Honor a world beyond pretense

In your cauldron heat passion cool
Avoid saying I was such a fool
Open to depths that bubble up
Honor the voice of your wisdom cup

Do you imagine what will follow action before doing or saying something?

5 CHANGE

Time for change and seeing
Life in balance for humans being
Listen to signals hear the calls
Countries politics slidings falls

Not written in black or red blood
Without mindfulness a coming flood
Cleansing washing unloading junk
Without renewal we're all sunk

Can immediate action reverse the ship
First an essential philosophical flip
Change in an instant turn on a dime
Status quo carries a crime

Heaven here why not understand
Creative ideas a source so grand
Among the blessed not a hard task
Many around look listen ask

Sweetest nectar for those who see
Eyes wide open don't let blindness be
Ecstasy calls in each passing breath
Your fate choose degradation or health

Are your responses adequate to calls for help?
What else can you do?

6 ACCOMPLISHMENT

Important get things done
Provides a sense you have won
On your face a big smile
Gone ambiguity for a while

Reminds what you can do
Allows pride born in you
Power control special tired too
Chases blahs when feeling blue

List checked feels good inside
Filling your sense of pride
Couch potato life for others
Not for my sisters and brothers

Each day an hour not so much
Added together it adds up
End of month end of year
Accomplishment pause cheer

Kaizen in Japan says it well
A little each day creates a big swell
Don't think much or cogitate
Get busy going out of your gate

How do you feel about daily activity and accomplishment?
Why is it important?

7 CALLING

Quickening now everyplace
Chaotic time for the human race
Take a chance stand be tall
Don't wait answer your call

Many say someone will save us
It is you are you brave enough
Power's internal don't wait on a guru
Face in the mirror there to serve you

Shoulder the task make community
There is strength in your unity
No savior or north star to guide
Your dear heart humanity inside

The race no dash to be won
Major commitment be as one
Stand on shoulders guiding the way
Wake god inside go out play

Hereafter you wait for here now
In every tree branch leaf cloud and cow
Night's not cold when you are held
Force in your field not a foe it's a friend

Do you hope for a rescue or savior or see yourself in that role?
How can you take more responsibility in your life?

8 FENCES

No time to straddle fences
Fail to act consequences
Turn left turn right
Glory or another fight

Scenarios dancing in brain
Evoke sun and thunderous rain
Life's balancing ball bounces up down
Leap to the stars crash with a frown

Answers at times a clear bell
At times choices havoc or hell
Do you know how to decide
To ensure god's on your side

What is your truth best answer
Keep plodding or become a dancer
Opportunity here no place to run
Cultivate mindsets have some fun

This or that doesn't matter
Concern is quieting mindless chatter
You're OK no matter direction
Heading home hold fast intention

Is there a payoff agonizing about perfect decisions?
How about either or knowing you can choose again?

9 UNION

Longing for sacred union
Connection protection engagement solution
Melding together meeting of minds
Human alignment without double binds

Roaring fire burning in hearts
Sharing many uncommon sparks
Roaring embers jump to flames
Sparking connection or dangerous games

Used to be easy you married that's it
Now a new game with a new twist
Not so easy life more complex
New values options sense of perplex

How to find your unique house
How to engage a prospective spouse
Where to find time where is the slice
A window to discover what's nice

What is the answer for your unique end
Are you still searching around the bend
Keep faith hold vigil do not go away
Clarity beckons inside do not stray

Trust inner guidance you have a plan
One foot then another you live again
There is a someone a gift sent your way
Hold heal cherish love them each day

*What is your self-talk about the loss of a sacred other and is your
mindset empowering?*
What is the state of your longing and how do you fill the void?
Might it be you?

10 FORGIVENESS

Now the time today the day
Let go of what gets in the way
So long fear good-bye resentment
One action to achieve contentment

About what you choose to do
Not what they put you through
Let go of holding set new intention
Lighten your load take new direction

Hanging on infects you
Firing endocrines blood boiling too
Impacts health and decisions
Eliminates revising revisions

Deconstruct this suggestion closely
Know it's about you mostly
Saying slowly the word forgiveness
Out comes the phrase for give ness

Here revealed truth of the matter
For give ness makes hearts pitter-patter
Takes care of you takes care of them
Get renewed start over again

Can you see forgiveness as letting go, a gift that enhances your health?
Do you realize it's a unilateral choice?

11 MORNING

Fortunate blessed watching sunrise
New beginning welling inside
Not only excitement anticipation
Chance for renewal sense of elation

Yesterday all washed clean
History just a sacred dream
Today a fresh page living rebirth
Clean slate creating new worth

Beauty inside arising to be born
No need to mope persist in forlorn
Red sky sun beckons you're alive
Out of the cave of your hidden hive

Dark night is closing good-bye so long
Morning thrown open sing a new song
When you're tired frustrated alone
Let promise of morning be a guide home

Let go thought forms binding like a vise
Good-bye anxiety it's rarely nice
Today a new day birthed in a new dawn
Today a beginning the real you is born

When was the last time you felt so alive it was a rebirth?
Do you know rebirth and renewal is a mindset you can choose?

12 ACCOUNTABILITY

Now no better time
Destiny calls life to the line
Fearful stomach hole in chest
Time for strength put forth best

Many moments take a chance
Grab the next rung do a new dance
Don't let opportunities pass by
Or sit on the doorstep ready to cry

Swallow deeply called by mission
No permission needed for sacred vision
No shrinking from responsibility
There's a brighter earth to see

Follow sparkles in your brain
Follow footsteps out of pain
Trust in heart song honor plan
Your future has a prideful I am

Reflect what was resistance about
Why so nervous without a shout
No worries if you did not possess
Skills and tools for happiness

What happened the last time you were called to take bold action?
Did you respond or let the moment pass?

13 PASSION

Now is all no time to waste
Look in the mirror now make haste
Lessons learned fill your presence
Well-schooled in your essence

Tools to make contribution
No delay you're a solution
No searching for perfect answers
Act now prevent disasters

Engaging in your daily job
What makes your heart throb
What calls with intense passion
For you to live in a new fashion

Legacy what gifts to leave
What serves others up your sleeve
Fail to share life locked inside
All you have hollow self-pride

Be careful of stories you tell yourself
Live your life don't be someone else
When leaving planet earth
Depart filled with joyous mirth

Are you living your passion?
How can you accomplish more and what would that be?

14 DOORWAY

Strong emotion grips sometimes
Sneaks up no rhythm or rhymes
Feeling empty deep in soul
Longing to fill an empty hole

Regardless of wisdom awareness grace
It shows up fills your space
Sometimes a specific cause
Sometimes from what once was

Sitting in sadness that is
Try sending away it's not your biz
It won't happen can't chase away
Can't rush ignore distract with play

Longing holds lessons pay attention
Its voice is giving direction
Listen to whispers inside
As a friend ally and guide

Heed direction it wants to take
Honor the message of your heartache
Trust the reality go deep explore
Follow as it leads to a door

What sadness are you experiencing?
What is the voice saying about something that needs doing or a relationship
needing healing?

15 BOLDNESS

Varied experience to fully live
Values reflect what you give
Noble actors on your stage
Your dreamscape to rearrange

Some constant cradle to grave
Familiar happenings rarely a wave
For adventurous souls on a path
Hard to predict the aftermath

Life unfolds note what's true
Don't deny feelings let them through
Honor emotions jumping out front
Deny them growth will stunt

You pay for mobility
A rich life rarely free
Remember where you come from
Mark heartbreaks battles won

Honor glory and your fears
Hold a vision from your tears
Never easy a path that's bold
Cherish memories growing old

What were the rewards and costs of proud things because you dove in?
Do you regret things you did or things you didn't do?

16 DREAMS

Life a dream state whatever that means
Engaged fantasy choosing what seems
What we're viewing we project
What we're missing our own neglect

Things we aspire things of pleasure
At our fingertips desired treasure
Each essence a deep core of light
You choose what you think right

Roar of greasepaint smell of crowd
Maintains focus perform proud
The core learning as we engage
Stay awake reflect and rearrange

Hearing footsteps of growing old
Fear for safety feeling cold
Risked your youth questing truth
Never could be locked in a booth

Aspiring always seeking ends
Also huddle with family and friends
Remember essence is a sacred dream
Never let go relish that stream

Is there is fixed objective reality or a collective dream?
What about control and free will?

17 STUCK

Gears stick get bogged down
Caught in a vortex leaving a frown
Need to move up down left right
Hard getting unglued stuck in fright

Longing resolution drives what we do
Voice of new vision makes music too
Indecision serves in a way
Included in the price we pay

Repeating voice clogs the mind
Time energy a challenge to find
Present pain not strong enough
In limbo till it gets too tough

Answers get caught in this vice
Only action will turn things nice
Take a step begin your return
Movement cools the frozen burn

In this challenging place of art
Voices make peace in your heart
Let silence teach as you learn
Trust responses honor the yearn

You have answers know what to do
Inner guidance carries you through
Careful mindless reactions and moves
Allow the wisdom of your own grooves

How do you process the dissonance when feeling stuck?
What voices do you listen to and follow and why?

18 STRETCHING

Giving caring loving them
Fill what's missing smile then
They're assured you will be there
Even though not physically near

Sit on fences project self
Giving to someone else
Look to fill an empty heart
Fill with light as a start

Joyous salvation you can't find
Making up your sweet mind
Recognize not one or other
In heart space all sister brother

Glory of you permeates deep
Pleasing others makes you weep
Rainbow at end lightens sky
Dazzling colors help you fly

Must you choose one or another
Would you deny sister brother
Love longs to find a feathered nest
Your own mind knows what's best

Love seek its end follow its tack
No control or holding back
Love as big as it wants to be
Honoring love sets you free

Has limiting the love you give served you?
What might happen if you gave more to many others?

19 SNOWING

Remember fresh fallen snow
Takes you to long time ago
Not sure why it quiets things
Inside snowfall silence sings

Stillness from an era when
World less manic simpler then
White gray swirls from a dull sky
Darkened quiet fills the eye

New snow invites opposites back
As we're seduced by a polar tack
As cold crisp air invites us out
We're drawn inside by a fire stout

Freezing chill a bracing delight
Look to the warmth of flannel at night
Labor shoveling heavy snow
Calls a slumber by embers' glow

Winters greeting of arctic bursts
Arouses one's tropical thirst
Snowfall is nature's treasure
Sprinkling flakes a heartfelt pleasure

What was the impact when you last experienced fresh snow and cold?
What does the memory hold for you?

20 PARTNERING

Agreements all over the place
Don't pay attention conflicts to face
Guiding grounding focus collaboration
Producing results beyond expectation

Expressing joint vision and a plan
Build trust with woman and man
Alignment enables states of grace
With the gift of agreement in place

Alone don't do much stumble about
Harnessed in tandem become stout
Hook up talents to a group with mission
Marvel the results of a shared vision

Partnerships grounded in covenant
Light you up with energy abundant
Connect with people at work
Be clear with loved ones don't be a jerk

Know what you are what you're about
Join with others stand back and shout
Amazed and thrilled with delight
Joyous teamwork makes life bright

Outcomes beyond what you had in mind
Life force of traction wells up you find
Satisfaction fills your heart
Joining others life becomes art

Do you have clear agreements with collaborators?
What do you notice about the relationship of clear agreements, conflict
and accomplishment?

21 ESSENCE

Sweet bubbling essence of you
Smiling face welcoming too
Giving yourself through life shifts
Arms open wide honor your gifts

Your source within your big win
No one takes it on another's whim
Honor in that sweet knowing
Opens the flow to divine growing

Fulfillment up on the surface
Living life purpose and service
Pure love filling inside
Knowing god walks at your side

Tears pain clean like a dove
Gone from life purified by love
After a while you know it's true
God's inside and outside of you

Carry on walking your path
Faith's elixir a soothing bath
Never alone with your bliss
Sweet heart holds you in a kiss

Do you know the strength and power you need is within?
How do you nurture and share that power, and what does it contribute to your
life and others?

22 ORDINARY

Ordinary life extraordinary ways
Filled with passion living ablaze
Honoring commitments caring for others
Those around are sisters brothers

No need notoriety or fame
Togetherness warmth without shame
Life simple easy content
Always sure you pay the rent

No majesty bright lights you as star
Equanimity happy where you are
Solid support for your whims
Earthly pride and wide grins

Blessings reach inside you
Soft tenderness comforts when blue
Children's voices sanctify the day
All platitudes melt away

No pretensions humble heart mind
Aspirations nowhere to find
Wisdom carried sustains everyday
Peace your presence so dance and play

What's really important to you?
What's the gap between here and where you want to be, and how can you
bridge it now?

23 REVERIE

Quiet essence of a sacred soul
Intense personal universal whole
Perspective quiets all longing
Centered source of early morning

Meditation as prayerful devotion
Quiet stillness roar of ocean
Some only quiet alone
Some dance evokes a plaintiff moan

Shared a common sacred force
Universal connection cannot divorce
Electric humming vibrates you
In the primordial bog life forces brew

Why periodically stop our glowing
Focused presence allows all knowing
See from a distance enjoy the view
Let go of personal it's not all about you

Accept outcome of endless searching
Connect your nature to your yearning
In reverie all drops away
Let spirit revel in gods play

What activities get you quiet and prayerful?
What does "gods play" mean to you?

24 MONEY

Money an energetic tool
Power rarely taught in school
Ticket opening doors
A reward there's always more

For some it is evil
Instrument of the devil
Opposite surely true
Think what it can do

All about your intention
It's neutral you add dimension
Reflects identity what you love
Can bring earth heaven above

Tool and friend for your mission
Aids many a sacred transition
Treasure a multiplying gold
Caretaker when you get old

No substitute for sacred love
Cannot buy caress of dove
Blessing when heart is pure
Gifts given to the poor

Not only financial assistance
Tool to overcome resistance
A form of bestowing grace
Salvation for the human race

If all freely bestow gifts
This planet can make shifts
Moving from want and greed
Abundance the end of need

Can you think of money as medium of exchange and tools for good?
How will you use yours?

25 SOURCE

Essential presence of power
Some have hour upon hour
Showing up centered in grace
Impact immediate on your face

Power is clean clear
No chatter easy to be near
Welcoming presence affirms being
Engages all promotes clear seeing

No pushing loudness or will
More yielding embodying still
Strong boundaries and none at all
Sometimes grand sometimes small

Source inside never put on
Not an illusion or quickly gone
Sometimes steel sometimes gas
Sometimes gentle sometimes sass

Manifestation from the core
Knowing what it's here for
A purpose a mission you trust
Can't derail does what it must

Drink the lessons it teaches
Listen to its voices reaches
Follow wisdom charisma charm
Knowing they will not bring harm

When you encounter a pure source
Celebrate presence honor its course
Bask in the glow of eternal flame
Let it burn away guilt and shame

Who do you know with personal power?
What is the impact and what do you emulate?

26 RESTING

Stuck frustrated feel a tightening grip
Get empty inside your quivering lip
No frantic digging when in this hole
Stop all flailing be home with your soul

Home a comfortable quiet state
No need of cameras to pan or gyrate
Trust surrounds no need for defense
Let down and be fully yourself

Place of resting no need for moves
Here you retreat to different grooves
You can stop thinking a relaxing place
Without production you bask in grace

Body relaxes breathing easier too
Familiar communion to sit and stew
Battlefield of life takes a warrior stance
Serving your mission demands you prance

Best work when your chatter subsides
Hearing your voice gods at your sides
Reverie enables connection to core
Quiet yields wisdom through a sacred door

Do you still access the presence available to you?
Do you know the ROI this presence represents?

27 INTIMACY

Connected to inner source
Authenticity the only course
Never fear seeming weak
Deepest heart let inside speak

Path to healing being close
Separation makes anxiety worse
Whatever pain and chagrin
Eats insides if you hold in

Surrender fully to dear others
Enable presence sisters brothers
Sharing essence in that way
Deepens the power of your stay

Let others know what's inside
No hiding in foolish pride
No sitting with pouting self
Engaging others is true wealth

Uncover what's inside
Navigate your personal tide
Thoughtful sharing never whim
Treasured wisdom from within

Is something weighing on you that needs authentic dialogue?
What is the risk reward of that conversation?

28 EMBRACING

Warm syrup flows within
Quiet mind no chattering chagrin
Silence black empty space
No concern running this race

Serene presence calming pure
Heart body mind aligned to ensure
Essence embraces those you hold
Daily giving never old

Uncover what's inside
Navigate your personal tide
Thoughtful sharing never whim
Treasured wisdom from within

Make sure family has peaceful sleep
Drying teardrops before they weep
Longing only to give take care
Helping others get to where

Peace from knowing who you are
Where you fit how you star
Integrity to the bone
In a crowd silence of alone

Perch you alight quiet perspective
Not from any outer directive
Sourcing wisdom from your soul
Agenda sometimes takes a toll

How would friends describe the essence of you?
Do you do work in the world around that best part?

29 EXPECTATIONS

Some have high expectations
Trust in divine revelations
Some never take a chance
Rarely ask someone to dance

When things don't go as expected
Grouse complain feel neglected
Proactive not part of the game
Just sit hope for fortune fame

Others make things happen
No hesitation no nappin
Never wait for sun to rise
Up early with stars in eyes

What gets under your skin
Ignites action for a win
Do you see vision a clear path
Through clouds to a warm bath

Challenged do you fold your tent
Waiting for things heaven sent
Create what you want to be
Manifest what you want to see

What describes you best
Sedentary or conquest
When things make you blue
Do you begin create new

Do you wait for things to happen or do you create the results you want?
What are you creating today?

30 SEEKING

Where I live
My emptiness wants to give
That wish a delight
After a lonely night

My lesson and struggle
Searches an empty bubble
I'm gifted this go-round
More still to be found

Soulful journey is my big quest
Longing seeking without rest
Older now wiser though
Seeker still wants to know

Path I travel up and down
Excited then a fretting frown
Joy escapes with a rush
Inward tears from the mush

I keep learning expanding breadth
Experiment operation of self
This process not for the meek
Seekers journey my cherished peak

What has your path been?
What has been your progress and what is the road ahead?

31 LEARNING

Human essence blessed in grace
Service honoring the human race
Drives awakening every day
Beneath challenges profound play

Dormant glory awakens a call
Here to there having a ball
Purpose to serve everyone
In that seeking there is fun

Beyond answers sacred truth
Sleuthing keeps us in youth
Sniffing solutions we're about
With our own blood-hound's snout

Taps the spirit of every cell
Discovery makes us swell
Deep satisfaction tall proud
Taking care of the crowd

Observe then you know
Learning makes juices flow
Cavorting on a meandering path
Wisdom becomes your sacred bath

What essence of humanity keeps us alive and exploring?
What learning engages you and why is it satisfying?

February

1 REINVENTION

Many lives one incarnation
Try personas test relations
Some steady narrow sphere
Others what's new this year

Unhappy things as they are
Not knowing what they're for
Who ego thinks you should be
Blocks essence from being free

Don't blame anyone else
Want different try a new self
If your way has you stewing
Time to begin renewing

Don't wait let go constraints
Create with fresh paints
No tears self-pity remorse
Chart a new path of course

Shed old skin leave it behind
Rotate cells leave worn behind
Peel the old show new face
Good-bye suffering hello grace

Have you made major changes in life?
What tools helped? Is it that time again?

2 SIMPLICITY

Quiet settled deep inside
Reason in a changing tide
Aspiration not driven for self
Serving god nothing else

Taking care in a time of mean
Empowering a heavenly machine
Miracles on earth every day
Turn to soar not ego play

Fear subsided vision clear
Quiet inside your good cheer
Receive now what you give
Make a choice how you live

No chasing acclaim reward
Materiality leaves you bored
Healing a challenged earth
Joyful quest of sacred birth

Hear a heart that openly sings
Cherish joy simplicity brings
No rat wheels block your way
Peaceful quiet serves each day

What visions do you hold for yourself, your country, civilization, the planet?

3 FAILURE

Failure a perspective
Careful of invective
Objective measure a fixed goal
Reaching not always a whole

Always value what you learn
Always more than short term earn
As you go here to there
Sometimes lessons not so clear

What's missing for you to do
What change in beingness too
Missed goals motivation
Success tomorrow a salvation

Fall short on your path
Resist your own wrath
Develop perspective context too
Easy on self talk it through

One step another play the game
Losing today no sense of shame
Critique failure so it's known
Pick up go temporarily home

Failure not getting knocked down
Failure staying on the ground
When low facing a cusp
Time to pick yourself up

No failure when you play
Fail only if you stay away
Whatever has important meaning
Engage fully presence beaming

What was learned when you did not reach a goal?
Did it inspire higher aspirations?

4 CREATING

Sourced by a drive to create
Make anew no template
Traveling places never been
Enduring loneliness within

Footsteps of advancing age
Harness existential rage
Give to those at your side
Through bumps and backslide

Longing driving pushing on
Directions you've never gone
Victory an impossible dream
Embrace process and a scheme

Know in your hidden recess
Exploring new is happiness
Always learning facing east
Each day a delicious feast

Creating growing is the thrust
Arise from inside if you trust
Follow voices deep inside
Innovation how we thrive

Where does your creativity come from and what is its impact?
What are the benefits of innovation and creativity?

5 RESURRECTIONS

What is your disease
Submerges and buckling knees
Disquiet without cease
Demands a search for peace

Challenge all along
Descent remaining strong
Unrest sleeps with you at night
Longing an ordinary predictable life

Can't ignore messages internal
Influence innermost kernel
In deep pools reflect this that
Always know where you're at

Going down for clarity
Within for more to see
Irritating since your youth
Searching for inner truth

Pain awakens from your dream
Revealing why you scream
Your mission here learning
Not consuming or needless earning

Awake immaculate being
To chasms of clear seeing
Surface with more self-respect
Thank voices from your depth

Each reconfigure rewiring tryst
Removes old shrouded mist
Reborn alive anew
Hear the blessings honoring you

Does the mission calm or create urgency?
Is being with missionaries helpful?

6 APPREHENSION

At times gripped by fear
Despite honors every year
This time land on our face
This time fall from grace

No matter success before
Or how often through a door
Is it real what we've done
To think we really won

Don't let me slide from favor
What forces will be my savior
Fear of tumbling from success
Need to transcend helplessness

Longing for something real
Alive and to feel
Fear part of the mystery
On the path to being free

Longing solace reverie real
Rest reflect with no keel
Apprehension motivator
Catalyze make things greater

Why fear no matter consistent success?
Irrational mind speaking, real impediments or motivations ?

7 QUIET

Silence no chatter or cracks
Serenity fills all your tracks
Would you last one more night
Awakened peaceful after long flight

Calm settles quieting fear
Anxiety suddenly disappeared
Longing for solace without agitation
Rest peaceful with seasoned elation

You've been through it every year
What moved you getting you here
Stopped dissipating energy
Embraced letting go to be free

Fear the culprit stealing space
Filling mind with disgrace
What to say about churning
Teaches us about our burning

Trust that wisdom prevails
Dampening today's travails
Courage step to the next rung
Faith provides a welcoming hug

How do you get to a place of quiet?
What do you do when access is challenging?

8 REKINDLE

Now is all no yesterday tomorrow
You have choice joy or sorrow
Sweet tears never go way
Stay home sulk go out play

Choose your experience
Beyond confusion or indifference
No world on a plate
Mud or oyster select fate

Sit alone wait for answers
Perfection a path to disasters
Stop fretting thinking worry
Quit babble choose with hurry

Tired of life looking glum
Things are bleak you want to run
Without perspective life seems black
Step back to get on track

Find a trajectory step into now
Muster power stand up somehow
Simple directions don't put them down
Honor their prodding please follow now

Do you have the will to change your state, perspective, mood and energy?
Can you make choices knowing you can choose again?

9 SATISFACTION

Awakens and quiets thirst
Respite from quests on earth
Revealing layers of your ken
Places you have rarely been

Present no place to go
No need of a rock n roll show
Opens hearts where you are
Jagged edges shining star

Sentient connected to source
Atonement no remorse
Chuckle quiet no tears in sight
Smiling takes you through the night

Sacred layers of your being
Expands presence focus seeing
Knowing gaze of clarity
Gone the trembling state of me

Warm light shines from within
Bathes pure spirit gone all sin
Blessings grace your sweet soul
Satisfaction of letting go

Are you satisfied with your inner life and progression?
What produced that and what are the next steps?

10 CHALLENGE

Awake in your life
Challenge what's ripe
Focus on where to go
Connect what you love so

Hours spent excited alive
All in then fully thrive
Allure of what turns you on
Grabs you awake at dawn

What attracts gives a smile
Choose a tack walk first mile
If not compelled by a vein
Keep looking don't complain

Choose favorite actions
Maximize tractions
OK to demand new
Visions that compel you

All around answers there
Strong voice say I am here
See beyond all disguise
Stop look listen open eyes

Is life filled with projects and people you are passionate about?
How can you generate enough in your life?

11 SNOW

Effort pushes each quest
Expend energy impress best
Contrast delivered for your eye
Needn't travel to get high

Powdered sugar sprinkled on all
Pristine landscape you stand tall
Nature brings a pure white view
No human effort nothing to do

Simple falling snow
Carefully listen already know
Not too much we chase fills us
Here what's needed to thrills us

No need run banter wave shout
All within rarely without
Wise oracle wisdom profound
To hear pearls quiet your sound

Beyond voices competing in time
Beyond chatter silent sublime
Beyond longings hungers pains
Beyond footsteps peaceful remains

Inside silent like fresh soft snow
Fluffy white cold makes you glow
Hello child delighting in rhyme
Exuberance feeds your divine

Awaken lacey beauty in you
Delicate presence supporting too
Honor sweets prowling your being
Luminous snow opens your seeing

Last time you felt divine presence?
What generated it and what prevents a regular occurrence?

12 COMPLACENCY

Cyclical drive to achieve
Hit a plateau get up leave
Vigilant if you want to achieve
Active cogent and believe

Malaise yields empty froth
No time to stall at the trough
Choose where actions at
Let things happen like that

Unconscious untracks aspirations
Don't give up your vibrations
World your oyster be the game
Talent commitment defines fame

Crumbled life beats you down
Changing smiles to a frown
Strutt your stuff don't run or hide
Eyes true north as your guide

Attractions pull awakened vision
For renewal no indecision
Momentum alive in your brain
Your umbrella shielding rain

What saps energy so you lose who you are and what you came to do?
How do you reclaim spark when off track?

13 GRACE

Knowing deepening heart
Profound caring exquisite art
Pure being here on earth
Lighten suffering spread mirth

Empathy for all in your space
Joyously foster sense of grace
Whatever habits whatever ill
Mission to melt stubborn will

Presence an honorable self
Can't be demanded by anyone else
Gifts freely given what you do
Takes nothing from and fills you

Joy observing smiles on their face
Want to enlighten the human race
Every journey starts at home
Don't forget you're not alone

Amazing how god cares for you
Ministering others trusting true
Remember secret for peace on earth
Quieting suffering a holy worth

How do you provide grace for others and how does it make you feel?
Are you generous or measured in giving your gifts?

14 LOVERS

Choose loves be smart
Conscious choices make life art
No expectations of receiving
Just give to the needing

For some about lust
No honoring adoring trust
Other's not to own possess
Not toys for your happiness

Giving freely nurturing growing
Allowing their fullness to flowing
Cherishing what passes between
Emerging creations now unseen

Seeing caring being there
Providing guiding being fair
Want all they can be on earth
Not to pleasure your self-worth

Present to what they need
Listen for what you might feed
Respect acknowledge presence
Promoting their profound essence

No matter distance or time
No matter reason or rhyme
Gift passes quickly pay attention
Enable love a noble dimension

Can you add more ways of loving others?
Who else can you love and how, including yourself?

15 WAKING

Striving pushing seems crazed
When awake from the dazed
Wherever mind was pushing to go
Abundantly clear you already know

No place to get why not be still
Deep in center find your strong will
From that quiet all does emerge
Clearest space after the purge

Much of life move frantically about
Demanding expecting ranting shout
Miss blessing of sacred being
Crashing through life without seeing

If lucky smart aware
Realize you are already there
No place to go or mountain to climb
Relax slide into your sacred rhyme

Centered within your sphere
Wisdom gets you to your next there
Bask in the reverie of your arrival
Nowhere to go nothing to strive for

Pure simple friends to flowers
Gentle steadfast hours upon hours
Confident radiant receiving clean
Enjoy pleasures of a magnificent dream

What if you're already where you're striving for and you had all you need?
If you were a human "being" how would your life be?

16 DECIDING

On the edge here or there
Feeling of getting nowhere
No grounding place of home
In a crowd all alone

Keeps you stagnant gripped
Never speaking tightly zipped
For others you have answers
Tell them how to be dancers

Want it all not miss a thing
Everyone everything
Let go allow get off the ground
Next perch there to be found

Given givens what to do now
To release your furrowed brow
Turn left center right
Walking long past midnight

No one has answers for you
Journey takes and gives too
Clear on knowns then decide
Trust instincts god's inside

Living in limbo a wicked curse
No bad choice cannot get worse
Not knowing its own hell
Recognize ring your bell

Time to make up your mind
Decide put it behind
If you find you chose wrong
Choose again sing a new song

What keeps you from making choices?
Do you know you can make another decision if you find that choice is now not
the best one?

17 CRISIS

Unraveling turning asunder
What do you think and wonder
Your status amid the plunder
Do you rage and thunder

What's the sense and perspective
Thoughtful or throwing invective
Leaders failed were they watching
Collapse while they were carping

Bedrock foundation assumed
Crumbled sand are you amused
Trusted narcissist dancers
Most only ego prancers

Committed to resolutions
Do you have sanguine solutions
Truth is no right answers
This path needs elegant dancers

Honor wisdom knowledge inside
In stressful times be your pride
Centered grounded honored voices
Action follows personal choices

What's the world around you and does it inform your choices?
Can you protect family, community, fortune, future?

18 STRESS

Not good for the constitution
Negative motivation not the solution
Mind spinning teeth grinding stomach knotted
Doesn't serve health manifest what's wanted

Fine line between tension and stress
Torque of tension pulls to success
Tension propels pushes you toward
Stress freezes in a tight wad

How do you tell where's the line
What might you do in your time
What's the action technique tool
Harness stress create a jewel

Progressing on your goals
Stuck in the mud digging holes
Wheels spinning over the line
Slow down rest drink fine wine

Find the solution works for you
Slow your process to see you through
Tension provides torque and action
Reward is exquisite traction

Can you feel tension when vision's out of alignment with where you're headed?
What destructive stress can you recalibrate?

19 COMPASSION

Deep inside under presence
Fundamental human essence
Beneath surface beyond reason
Emergent response to treason

Rage a memory primordial fear
Terror of birth injustice here
Rises up if crossed or burned
Violations pleading spurned

Reactivity rips things apart
Contrast a compassionate heart
Forgo devilish blood revenge
Or risk suffering spiteful edge

Use intensity grow a stronger heart
Accelerate the human art
Reservoir of this powerful force
Energy from a profound source

Trespass poisons a compassionate soul
Violate them makes you less whole
Beckon caring love sweetness more
Your soul births what you came for

See betrayers needing your love
Needing warmth not a shove
Respond in compassion not vitriol hate
Ticket through an evolutionary gate

What triggers and taps into your rage?
Next time ask what is there to learn and transmute energy into something
that resolves?

20 BLESSINGS

Voice of complaint chatters loud
Speaks from right and proud
Always flaws all around
Fails to see beauty surrounds

Wrong this wrong that
See what's missing let us chat
Righteous indignation wells inside
Serving separation feeding pride

What sources negative perspective
Making others' objects of invective
Glass half empty glass half full
You choose the frame lever to pull

Humble suggestion can you see worth
Notice the blessings here on earth
Count the goodness every day
Sky sun ocean magic at play

Food from the ground touch of a lover
Spark of a kiss mind deep in wonder
Tears of the heart honor a friend
Laughter always is just ahead

Surly voice starts to pitter patter
Chase grumblings that do not matter
Embrace infinite lovely surroundings
Live for joy and blessings abounding

What can you discover about perspective from your thinking habits?
Can you count blessings consistently and see beauty, miracles and lovely people?

21 JOURNEY

Takes you places near and far
To contemplate realms ajar
Inner outer high and low
Dark pathways sometimes glow

Doing being having to
Lead and follow every you
Journey has you smile and scream
New heights to a shattered dream

Not what happens but response to
On the road who rides with you
Wisdom in every leaf and drop
On wind and stream and every crop

Bounty of each curve and bend
Teaching beauty beginning to end
Treat things lightly let heaviness go
Not up or down but how you grow

Get back the giving paid in kind
Driving grander than your mind
Internal peace value supreme
Courageous faith honors your dream

Careful false gods charlatans fake
Never beauty do not give they take
Follow heart maps burning inside
Wise voices with magic in their stride

As time grows quiet sensing end
Double closeness to each friend
Join creatures of sea feathered too
Humble lenses see no less than you

Do you speak about your life journey with judgment or reflection with learning,
honoring and creativity?

22 EXPANSION

Who are you when all goes away
In your room what do you say
What presence when alone
What about on the phone

We get bigger with another
Very large with a lover
Around the table where you sit
Presence grows when you're with

Front of a room in command
Bordering on being grand
In a hall even bigger
Though fear makes you quiver

In a stadium must expand
Project like a marching band
Small voice inside magnified so
Message empowers as you grow

Unique presence drawn by others
Holiness coaxed by sisters brothers
Never know who you might be
Let courage inspire then you see

Who are you with others, how do you show up in different contexts?
What moves being bigger than you think?

23 ETERNAL

Does your heart rest in peace
Can it let go of fight be with ease
Beauty emerges from that place
As your essence embraces grace

No pretense or filtered you
In a place of flow old and new
No joy when toiling life away
Without a place to slow and play

To capture who you are
Let observers see the sparkling star
Eternal essence does not say or do
It's holy rhythm is the solace that's you

Do you have a place where you let go and be?
Do you understand stretching is about letting go, not efforting?

24 SELF-POSSESSED

Who are you how do you be
What self reflects all your me
Do roots hold you to earth
Provide an anchor of self-worth

Self-assured what you're about
Stalwart inside ballast stout
Center took years of work to entrain
Reflecting essence beyond your brain

Nothing hidden traveling your path
Foster unfolding your soft grass
Energy pouring from your cells
Entering a room light rings bells

Awakened enlivened tempered to bone
Such a clear presence so pure the hone
Empty of anger released at source
Inner wisdom guides you forth

Others see integrity within
Know you're not a creature of whim
Rarely regretful no sense of should
Reflective presence nourished by good

How do you feel about the presence you are and how are others reacting?
What changes are needed?

25 NAVIGATING

Hard drive spinning out of control
No sense of being whole
Thinking gnashing all not knowing
Cannot keep machinery going

Compass was not guiding to port
Time to divine your true north
Look to core for the next tack
Answers to get you back on track

Pretending you don't know
Self-deception blinds so
Beyond fear responsibility
To discern your real me

Stuck can't locate center
Get quiet find a place to enter
Ask what if you knew
Trust response your god is true

Manifest all your gifts
Navigate internal shifts
Harvest time not being weak
Sometimes strong being meek

You have answers know the way
Remember always one more day
Observe what others project
Don't be afraid self-protect

How do you find center when lost?
Since never really lost what's useful self talk about your temporary state?

26 DOWN

Loose ends inside out
Evoking screams and shout
Earnest expectations high
Fallen shattered want to cry

Suddenly feeling the end
Not excited by your trend
Mission of change high hope
Now a great sense of nope

Each time descend this hole
Hard to climb out rescue your soul
Strength resolve cannot muster
Cannot get by on blarney bluster

Great expectation vision you hold
Daring bravado making you bold
Courage gone fear quiet cold
All you want someone to hold

Hope faith waning resolve low
Critical moment reflect grow
Time for what's needed here
Learning kindness caring to share

When down do you explore the cause or power through?
What valuable lessons have you received from deep sadness?

27 PRAYER

Where turn when all seems lost
Warmth elusive all's in frost
Mind cloudy presence fogged
Can't breathe airways clogged

Deepest recess of desire
Longings you aspire
Dark covered in night
What solace makes things right

You have a center pure being
Turn there when need to cling
Place of worship statue poem
A person you call home

Holy union of I and thou
Fills the dark soothes somehow
Raging beast churning wild
Quietly embraces inner child

Still calm go to that place
Drink it in with sage of grace
Present thru each travail
Holding keeping you prevail

Where do you turn when all is swirling?
Do you have a practice, how does it feed you, what else do you need?

28 LOST

Heavy sad weight on my bones
From the top of my head filling my toes
Molasses clogs every pore
Heart screams can't take anymore

How'd this happen what's the curse
Hole in heart cannot get worse
Eyes tearful wetness red burn
Where is solace which way to turn

Something's missing a broken heart
Mystery attacks each fresh start
What resources fund new life
One that sustains no screeching strife

What guidance to a new place
Pasture of sweetness slice of grace
Giving strength to walk in light
Pick self up set new sight

Grant me courage wisdom and such
To get beyond shame feeling so much
Want to be here stay on this earth
Need help resurrection and a rebirth

How have you been betrayed and betrayed yourself?
Anyone beside you need an apology and what changes will regain congruence?

29 WANDERLUST

Beginning a new unraveling
Inside wants to be traveling
Feelings I've felt before
Going through another door

Journey ahead not looking joyful
Bubbling up teary mournful
Darkness calling not inviting
Saying please no more fighting

I keep busy meeting greeting
Provide comfort help and seeding
Endless promoting not my longing
Prefer respect innovation belonging

Yearning inside to be joyous
Stillness eludes feeling porous
Endocrine overload no rhythm rhyme
Churning burning not fun this time

Seeking peace soon the future
Deeply grounded family nurture
Needing connection and county
Ernest roots precious bounty

What grounding does connection provide and why is it important?
Do you honor those who provide it for you?

March

1 SHARING

When windows open use vistas well
They light a course hear all they tell
Honor beauty revealing itself
Welcome the divine let go all else

Sow from your godly source
No energy on petty remorse
Bounty's your nature service your being
Abundance joy happiness freeing

Choose now nothing holds you back
Heading down your noble track
Go forth propagate progeny abound
Serve a mission keep moving around

Thoughts dwelled on fills their mind
Chatter as wisdom keeps them blind
Some evil selfish afraid
Of only mind how do I get paid

Wake lead them from selfish hell
Use words wisely teach lessons well
Discover what you're made of
Holy blessed vibrate your love

What lessons are you here to teach?
Is your path enabling that or do you need to make course corrections?

2 SPRING

Awake alive whirring stirring
Springtime and we're all buzzing
Winter's doldrums chilly nights
Spring brings energy flights

We forget when spirits low
Life comes around stay in flow
Seasonal pattern up down
First smile then a frown

Not only seasons follow this call
Internal passages rise and fall
Remember in hibernation
You're reborn new celebration

Daisies poppies carnations roses
Flower again beautiful poses
Nourishing rain cleanses your soul
Up and down so we roll

Without fallow times within
Never wear your next grin
When buried in a slumber cold
Quiet still spring will unfold

When fallow is it difficult to remember things are cyclical?
Can you remember winter produces value?

3 DIRECTION

Closed loop brain spinning round
Repeat echo same droning sound
Words inside a private curse
Thinking could not be worse

Internal chatter churning again
Always half empty never a win
Poisoned treadmill stuck on a tack
Voice inside machinegun flak

Pushing forward addictive quest
Voices pounding never rest
Sitting in smugness ego fed
Longing for solace cozy in bed

Thinking life will not improve
Eternal sentence stuck in a grove
Craving new different perch
Place that's home is your search

You keep striving onward bound
Voice inside a repeating sound
Spinning bubbling bucking brews
No matter accolades you say lose

Suddenly let go of the voices call
Something rescues in free fall
Seeing graces with perspective
New way of being new directive

When stuck was it an external event or an internal shift that moved you?
Can you create that shift if needed?

4 TERROR

Anxious tight clenched jaw
Teeth grinding slamming door
Brain chatters loudly with speed
Incessant fear
hides what you need

Mercury retrograde heart aflutter
Sometimes for you sometimes another
Uneven breathing marks passing time
Suddenly stop take air for a while

Why this agitation
Unknown future without elation
Frightened child lives within
Likes routine where it's been

Adult ego questing spirit
Takes us places stretching limit
Preparing for the journey ahead
Playing scenarios expectant dread

Terror of failure death of a kind
Reeking havoc torturing mind
Good news learn to resist
Allow treasures in your midst

Learn to check negative thinking
Let go of thoughts without blinking
Create the world in your mind
Leave the negativity behind

How has fear stood in your way robbing your experience?
Why not do "it" anyway?

5 DECIDING

Beyond turmoil randomness of dice
Launching new space expecting rice
Free of cogitation old migraine brain
Time for action all that remains

Primal indecision had you vise gripped
Afraid of choices fear of being gypped
Baffling options repeat back then forth
Aqueous fluids whipped into froth

Suddenly cheerful out of the tube
Your ears were full now time to groove
Dark clouds dispersed after torrential rain
Lightening enabled letting go of pain

Doing easy once you know what
Deciding the hard part casting your lot
Freedom waiting so make a choice
Begin celebrating you can rejoice

Always remember if you choose wrong
Choose again sing a new song
Precious effort not wasted for naught
Every decision lessons are taught

How much have you suffered making decisions?
How has learning from decisions informed current behavior?

6 PRIDE

Sense of pride when complete
Accomplishment very neat
Beginning you didn't know
End result so you gave it a go

Taking on something worthy
Will it go topsy-turvy
Create mish mash big mess
Miss a chance for happiness

Perhaps OK for your hearing
Others engage get their bearing
Deeper in whatever it is
Realize traction wow gee whiz

Seeing completion in sight
Just might be dynamite
Suddenly on the other side
You say wow what a ride

Everyone pulled from inside
Allowing all to fill with pride
Anticipating a new quest
Recall what you did best

What fears about your meaningful work holds you back?
What generates faith and trust?

7 GOD

Force energy without within
Holds all together often a grin
Takes care always on watch
When we itch it's the scratch

Unsteady ready to crack
Always god at your back
Where to turn when scared
Solace when soul bared

Faith fleeting energy low
Unconditional god's love flow
Compassion gets you through
In your trauma god gives to you

Friend in emergency time of need
Shining knight on a trusty steed
Grace filled portal there to lead
Any challenge any deed

Glorious kingdom there for you
God the essence waiting for you
Don't wait tap into the source
God's love enfolds without remorse

How do you hold the idea of god: person, ideal, energy, set of rules, love?
Is it your perception or someone else's?
Do you have a personal understanding and knowledge of God?

8 RESILIENCE

Life has moments up down
One day royalty next a clown
Message in all the haze
Success demands being brave

Answer to winning your game
Keep going infamy or fame
Lesson on your trip
When you fall only a blip

Get slapped in the face
Other cheek heat of the race
Get up stay down
Stand tall rarely frown

Simple refrain get up again
Engage each morning then
Quality thinking keeps you on track
Not all you do it's how you act

Choose to stay in the game
Correct missteps try again
Ribbons await a resilient soul
Bounce again refuse acting old

Last time you were knocked down what did you think and how did you react?
How did you get from there to where you are?

9 REFUGE

Where to run and hide
Escape pain inside
Head spinning breath shallow
Terror in my marrow

Emptiness hole in gut
Always falling in this rut
Where's the exit door
Freedom my heart longs for

Motivation not for now
Wondering if ever how
Will a bullet quiet the pain
Is that sentence a worse rain

Longing clear quiet inside
Knowing there's no place to hide
Stifle chatter deal with pain
Make a plan start again

Refuge in your compassion
Beyond self-loathing your passion
Deep in quiet empty stillness
Wisdom solace and forgiveness

What is the source of pain that disturbs a sense of peace?
What are the gifts of demons buried in suffering?

10 QUEST

Clean clear vibration no static or goop
No wings flapping in your inner coop
Inquiry's over searching ceased
Effort quieted your hungry beast

Longing midwifed ground searched for
To get there opening door after door
Reverberating thoughts in your brain
Kept you questing till no doubts remain

When you decided your choices made
Thru the misgivings and sense of shame
Who did you hurt what did you let go
In pushing forward having to grow

Goal of the effort expanding your health
Did you let go and move to new wealth
Can you slip into new skin with ease
No wake or displacement does this pool please

Lying down at the end of long days
Can you grin knowing you've come thru haze
Carrying forward are you without remorse
As growing confidence keeps you on course

When you say yes to the above
You earn knowing nods from forces of love
Let faith and wisdom continue your ride
As you enjoy gliding with pride

What have you given up in search of integrity for what rewards?
Any advice for others who followed their heart at great personal cost?

11 LIGHT

Sparkling vibrations in space
Scenes give life face
Vibrant colors pleasing eye
Sometimes laughter sometimes cry

Beauty not always perceived
Seeing what's believed
Our view always filtered by
Light in portals reflect mind's eye

Allow what you want to know
On your screen to help you grow
Glory available beyond dreams
As well as death door screams

Sacred profane much offered you
Enhancing experience sometimes blue
Realize the contrast defines sight
Up informs down dark birthing light

Project white light be a forceful haven
Outshine places projecting craven
A beacon of good bright clear intention
Channel goodness without self-rejection

Let sparks within find their expansion
Grow multiply inside your mansion
Let your path be pure compassion
Serving to guide no matter fashion

Reflect on the view of outside source
Let integrity be your favored boss

*Do you make conscious choices about what you take in and what you put out?
What is the opportunity in choices you make for creating your inner and
outer world?*

12 RECOGNIZING

No greater joy celebrating others
Bask in glowing sisters brothers
Recognize genius applaud pure being
Acknowledge gifts you are seeing

Moving forward sense of mission
Centered with a clear vision
Putting smiles on others face
Powerful exuding grace

Art of another in their essence
Energy flows in their presence
Not about learning studying will
Comes from their core tranquil

Elegance in music dance design
Engineering architecture media so fine
Stop for a moment appreciate art
Pause reflect on the song of a heart

You may not love the creation
Though you know it came from elation
Traversing the paced life you live
Stop celebrate the way they give

Are you impacted by the divine in other's creativity?
How about your creativity and how it touches others?

13 DESTINY

Silence no chattering mind
Noisy chorus left behind
Expectation of your lover's kiss
Soaring heavenly promise of bliss

Words dancing in brain
Synapses connect play a refrain
Waiting for you to be kind
Joy wanted hoping to find

How to know pathway is clear
Road emerging grins ear to ear
Is this channel a guide you need
Heaven sent providing god speed

Encounters unravel a layer of dust
Beyond resistance step into trust
Follow heartbeats heeding your rhyme
Delay patience in this quickening time

Pure joy of living quiets your mind
Yesterdays challenges recede behind
Honor trajectory time and space
You are blessed with elegant grace

Meeting destiny unscathed unbowed
Pinnacle rises above the crowd
Brass ring quested so many years
Grab it now beyond tears and fears

What do you do to quiet your monkey mind and become a mindful observer?
What value will mastering the chatter bring?

14 LIFE

Great journey called living
Challenges joy giving receiving
Dear ones smile hearts aflutter
Disappointments cause a shutter

Over many bumps on the road
Mindset helps carry the load
Sometimes lose it let go let fly
Can't hold tears have a good cry

Joyless sadness empty within
Hollow vessel wreaks havoc then
Convinced you cannot take more
Calling provides an enlivening chore

Remember before making a fuss
Life's about learning not about us
Lessons engendered by elation's pain
Each one makes you whole again

Minds' eye holds keys to happiness
Careful of measures defining success
Be observing see everyone else
Not all serious laugh at yourself

Do you get engaged in life's day to day drama?
Have you tried seeing from a higher altitude larger perspective?

15 BIRTHDAY

Each year an anniversary of birth
Reflect blow candles check our girth
Communicate with those we love
Share essence thank gods above

Opening eyes to truths of our life
Longing for quiet freedom no strife
Searching for home keys fit locks
Belonging under nooks and rocks

Plans for future dance in our head
Vision next week month years ahead
Clarifying purpose closer to source
Measure activities avoid remorse

Drinking in beauty moving with grace
Using self-talk to slow the pace
Standing in sweet air perfumed by roses
Lingering attention of poetry and proses

Taking time to tell those connected
Their presence keeps us resurrected
Rejoice celebrate humbly honor
Those serving us like mother and father

Do you mark the milestones of life partying,acknowledging, reflecting or all?
How have changes made after reflection been useful?

16 DOORS

Sometimes a struggling fight
Have a vision you know right
Search for words to express
Seeking listeners will say yes

Compelling images pull to act
Sometimes thrash on a wrong tack
Go back reflect set new clarity
Chart a course on current reality

Begin again not quite right
New listeners bring uncertainty fright
One day breakthrough struggle no more
No banging heads you find the door

There all the time somehow shrouded
How it works when you're clouded
Clear as a bell emerge from your mist
No longer frustrated no inner tryst

Engaged conversations broadcasting news
The world an oyster you get to choose
Do not give up on your quest
Keep going find your happiness

Life is discovering what satisfies you and surrounding yourself with it.
Are you doing that?
What's in the way?

17 PRIDE

Task we face wandering earth
Remaining true to sacred birth
Story unfolds each day we live
Get from life what we give

Compassion the highest art
Human essence live from heart
Joy of life continually learn
Beyond how much you earn

After years on the planet
What legacy will you leave on it
Find great joy giving to others
Sharing time with sisters brothers

Reflect on years develop pride
Go through life little to hide
Take no more than you give
Remember always to forgive

Life holds much if you trust
Have faith enjoy laugh and lust
Food on the table pay the rent
In the end it's heaven sent

Spend more time thinking about getting or giving?
What provides real satisfaction and what is the best way to get that?

18 RENEWAL

Primordial scream ripped heart
Hole in belly sets you apart
Voices of wisdom do not work
Shameful alone no prideful smirk

How did you get here how to get back
Do you deserve feelings so black
What antidote for heartfelt remorse
How can you end a winter of loss

Body is listless soul so blue
Emptiness loneliness pervading you
No time to hide no time to fear
This has been brewing many a year

Where do you take your tragedy
How to rebuild an identity
Where are sages to help with pain
Where is shelter from pounding rain

Where is the outcome that serves
While quieting raw fragile nerves
Where to find solace after you've wept
Is there a map or tentative step

One says withdraw another engage
Listen for wisdom inside tears and rage
Sorry no answer to find outside
Place for direction the voices inside

From a dark hour new sense of worth
Time now to flower ahead a rebirth
All is in cycles down to know up
Phoenix will rise filling your cup

Do you have unhealed pain?
What does your wisdom say about resolution and wholeness?

19 CONSUMPTION

Times are changing Mr. Dylan said
No turning back yesterday is dead
Lives in the balance added Jackson Browne
Choice people have go up go down

Energy talent heartfelt desire
People need freedom and will to conspire
Nothing to lose no downside or risk
Embolden empower without a fist

Internal fighting demands cunning smarts
Find buried answers in golden hearts
Get beyond stories lies we've been told
Falsehoods deceptions not to be sold

Without stuff they sell we're all ok
Leave junk on shelves to rot away
Don't need sellers stories myths dreams
Heart minds expire without better memes

Know what to do what to think and say
No more false truths to stand in your way
No more false gods with guileless shame
Or naked emperors worthy of blame

How much of a consumer are you?
Do you buy stuff mindfully?
What about TV advertisement?

20 RELEASING

Holding old visions and lives
Careers homes not the prize
Fresh starts without old weight
Going forward new template

Unforgiving scenarios old
Wrapped in shackles binding hold
Blinders surround the possible now
Cloud new vistas constraining how

What's seen shaped by who's looking
What's served reflects who's cooking
Reinvention what you need
Old ego ties will impede

Something good in continuity
Folks around provide congruity
Need not be blood profession race
Spiritual family takes their place

Mental walls are only clay
No need to hold yourself at bay
Careful ghosts clouding precision
What's your message what's your vision

What barriers do you construct for yourself and how do they constrain?
How can you stop?

21 FREEDOM

Suddenly flat without chatter
Complaints gone no matter
Visions for tomorrow clear
What you want already here

No shattering noise dissonant sound
All is quiet no longer bound
Crippling programs of yesterday's mind
Fading receding all left behind

Yesterday's storms you have weathered
New freedom being untethered
Monsters conquered chased or dead
Purged from awareness now a clear head

What resides inside you
Now you're empty no longer blue
What do you say every day
Providing direction new sense of play

Messages are loud and clear
Let go attachments no holding dear
All's transitory it shifts and moves
Let go irksome find your own grooves

Don't fight the river float downstream not up
Life's not a struggle please fill up your cup
Be even serene observe all that passes
Rise above understand engage in life's classes

What thinking habits are you holding that no longer serve?
What words affirm and serve who you are now?

22 IMPRINTING

Shapes who you are how you be
Limits how fast and far you see
Programed before you knew much
Conversations listening and such

What is the imprint of DNA
How much biology governs our way
Holds generations to what it might be
Biological ancestry of its unique tree

Not only genetic loading
Impact of other's presence foreboding
In through senses and pores
All before we develop walls

Arrives thru genes words energy
Limits capacity of being free
World views influence who we are
Till we rise above cannot get far

If not getting where you want to go
Can't figure out what's holding you so
Cleanse the thoughts planted in you
They impinge what you say and do

Childhood words others use
Can narrow what you peruse
Honor yourself gain full height
Reprogram words worldview fright

Let go restrictions you did not choose
Chase their values you won't lose
To manifest your unique vision
Cleanse imprints that imprison

How would your life be different if you reprogrammed after
consciously choosing
your own values, beliefs and worldviews?

23 SERVICE

Arrived shared made many friends
Purposeful meetings with noble ends
Seekers healers with common mission
Honoring tradition heralding transition

Suffering alone on separate paths
Learning what triggers personal wraths
Must be the change you seek
Substantial effort not for the meek

Doctors lawyers priests leading edge
Stand tall on values out on your ledge
It's reeling spinning listen the yelp
Humanity needs your help

Those you serve impact many lives
They're hurting searching fed up with lies
Seek what's enduring a calling to serve
Come with presence perseverance and verve

Seek to restore what's missing on earth
Remember you came to contribute worth
Time to rise up create new story and vision
Act quickly with resolve and precision

Time to lead colleagues and friends
Time to honor thoughtful ends
Engaging with prayers and dreams
Honoring service to higher things

What is your calling and what legacy do you want to leave?
What institutional constraints that impact your service need to be addressed?

24 BREAKTHROUGH

On a personal verge
Step forward exhibit nerve
World not a frightening place
Opportunity to express grace

Tears shed roar with laughter
Focus on a compelling after
Learn lessons source of wisdom
Grow from beauty in them

We all need absolution
Preparing for a next solution
Never perfect at times cruel
Sometimes caviar sometimes gruel

Nearing breakthroughs you need
Will coming years bring more greed
Have enough to meet needs
Have more time do good deeds

Beyond a problem mind set
See what's here and yet
Challenge for one and all
Learn think no need fall

Essentials surround us here
Potential bliss little fear
Live in a grateful way
Count blessings sit and pray

How do you know challenging situations are problems?
Can you see them as opportunities to develop wisdom?

25 CLEANSING

Scrub where consciousness dwells
Cleanse the detritus of your cells
More than brains need wiping clean
Chemistry impacts our being

Many techniques abound
Choose one you think profound
Yoga provides release supreme
Religion may satisfy your dream

Strenuous exercise quiets chatter
Wisdom schools share their matter
Wilderness hiking silent meditations
Regressions and chanting incantations

Practices are a proven mean
Creating minds that are clean
Clarity wisdom in everyone
No installation ready to run

Quest for insight enlightenment
Search and find where it went
Always with you needs dusting off
Employ your master jeweler's cloth

Have practices that reboot your system?
Why not do it often and make it a practice in your life?

26 GRACE

Search for meaning connection grace
Hunting longing seeking a place
Speaking to this one that one who knows
Looking for answers in all sorts of prose

Exhausted from running around
Fear home will never be found
When sure you cannot win this race
Destiny lifts you into grace

Longing results from internal divorce
Finally plug into your central source
Suddenly connection within
Footsteps encircle a place to begin

Placing your answers outside yourself
Putting reliance on somebody else
Constant deferring leads to disasters
Brothers sisters do not have your answers

Stand tall step into pride
Know your guide alive inside
Consult your private god
As you recieve a knowing nod

Have you discovered the source of power in your core that guides your life?
What challenges has it presented, what learning has it facilitated?

27 DELIVERANCE

Life evolves never static
For animals not problematic
Roll with changes no resist
No storms just some mist

Humans different we have mind
With stories of what's left behind
Fuss agitate anxiety rules
Countless hours being fools

White knuckles resist changes
Fight gravity as world rearranges
Static we lock up quickly
Pray for rescue feeling icky

How great yesterday was
Looking back creates buzz
Opportunity knocking at the door
Say we don't want anymore

Then complain we are stuck
At last see can't pass the buck
Take responsibility for your station
Deliverance knocks say yes with elation

What form is your resistance and how good are you at transcending?
What value has resistance provided and what cost?

28 ADVENTURE

Life lived well infinite choices
Opportunities celebrations rejoices
Creativity inside unleashed roars
Intentional directed experience soars

Whatever tack heart song says go
Beauty manifested yours to sow
Enjoy richness landscapes unseen
Allow abundance from your dream

Maintain courage undaunted by pride
No doubting yourself heed voices inside
Follow wisdom the quiet voice within
Allow its strength indulge its whim

Places you get to inside and out
Tickle heartstrings making you shout
When you're nervous frightened scared
Remember it's never that bad

You cannot see where you'll end up
Trust have faith exploit your pluck
Live your life from inside out
Inner guidance knows the best route

Do you have a good relationship with your inner guidance, honoring it's wisdom and directions? What mitigates and what promotes trusting the voice?

29 DIRECTION

Keeping an extraordinary pace
Despite all the doing in this race
Fast to disaster nowhere a compass
Realize its' chaotic rumpus

Searching a page with no direction
No instructions for reflection
Seeing movement without traction
Someone asks what motivates action

With chagrin time to get clear
Going without knowing ends up anywhere
Have poise thru noise create a treasure
Bestowing gifts of great pleasure

With intention of a noble goal
Direction helps staying whole
No blink or wink on the course
Steadfast becomes a profound source

Do you have clarity about life direction or are you blown around?
What criteria do you use to evaluate if you are truly on a path??

30 ANTICIPATION

Vision for a life to be born
Wakes you up at dawn
Restful sleep eludes
Joy excitement exudes

Looking to what lies ahead
Expectant visions keep us fed
Savor moments now 'til when
All the time elated and then

Time the trickster already there
Though mind tells us we're here
Time a story learned long ago
Most take literally we all know

Truth all happened long ago
Only now you have consciousness so
Savor it now savor it then
When it's now savor again

Realize it's not what you do
Being brings life to you
Trust have faith forgive let go
Let precognition increase love's flow

*Do you manifest the future making choices, decisions and actions or do you rely
on instinct?*
Is that working?

31 NOW

This moment is the answer
Why suffer minds disaster
Your work your task
Cherish life find serenity bask

Tormented life of your mind
Not real makes you blind
Present to observing observer
Detachment takes you further

Forward step allow presence
Tap your core reveal essence
Feeling friction pain delusion
Monkey mind creates confusion

Ticket to joy of expansion
Breathe deeply in your mansion
Not the past or hope for tomorrow
Be in now nothing to borrow

On your feet savor pulsation
Expand with power your vibration
No deference to old voices and ghosts
Step forward to become your most

Can you be in this moment without a sense of past or future?
Can you be without the limiting power of fear?

April

1 LETTING GO

Wars judgments raging in you
No longer blaring you're free and new
Let go busyness of yesterday's mind
Step into new life leave all behind

Windows wiped squeaky clean
Life dream merged with being
Once dark clouds and rain
Now sunshine releasing pain

Trust and seeing magnified many fold
Suddenly wiser mystic from old
Much more playful a child emerged
Admonitions prohibitions guilty shame purged

Through this window see all around
Ecstatic presence awakened in sound
Voices of eons calling to you
Everything taking on a new hue

No chatter clouding your now
Ego silenced on your clean prow
Raining light empowerment from above
Embrace and accept that sacred love

Does your mind chatter represent something incomplete?
Would life be different if noise was resolved?
What might you do?

2 EDEN

Eden here on earth
All around gift of birth
Bird songs glowing moon
Shining sun laughing loon

Running streams dancing rain
Reaching corn flying crane
Told by powers that could
Earth endured heaven good

Why keep heaven from all
Heaven's here no need to fall
Not the fastest computer or toy
Not a job new suit smart ploy

Are you willing to see
Wake the love in you and me
Heaven is the heaven you are
Lies just beneath not very far

No need climb descend take flight
Be still calm quiet your fright
Despite the driving need to earn
Love within fills every yearn

Do you appreciate the power and joy of loving kindness in yourself?
What would change if you brought love and compassion to others?

3 AGREEMENTS

Agreements are all over
Without them you're a rover
Implicit framing collaboration
Explicit results beyond expectation

Shared visions set a clear plan
Build trust for woman and man
Alignment and agreements in place
Easier to reach states of grace

Accomplish little alone
Harnessed together stronger than stone
Hook talents to a team with a mission
Results flow from expressed joint vision

Partners with a deep covenant
Light you up in energy abundant
Solid ground with your team
With loved ones express a dream

Know who you are what you're about
Align with others stand back shout
Be amazed with great delight
Teammates make your life bright

Results beyond what you had in mind
Life force wells up without any bind
Satisfaction fills your heart
Joining with others life becomes art

What conversation do you have to get an explicit shared vision
before you trust and move forward?

4 CONFIDENCE

Why not engage today
Let what I cherish come my way
Not just transient to get
Deep-seated wants to never fret

Life offers joy at the core
Take care of basics need little more
Price you paid in reflection and search
You get to sit on your perch

Sitting with a clear mind
Frustrations gone left behind
Trust what lies deep inside
Share that gift as you glide

Go forth continue the search
Nothing wished beyond this earth
Desires for others may be rich
For yourself only a pinch

Glory here no need waiting
No holding back or hesitating
Expend all give for free
No expectation it comes back you see

Do you appreciate where you've been and what you learned?
What do you lose in giving without expectation?

5 ENOUGHNESS

Awaken dance jubilantly
You're enough celebrate your me
Nothing to prove no badges to earn
After all your striving time to turn

Gaping hole filled with delight
Whatever mania gone sleepless night
Missing ingredient driving each quest
Time to let go you earned a rest

For the work selflessly done
Enjoy the rewards you finally won
Many choices you could've made
You chose a path with a steep grade

Reflect on your daunting race
Bask in your deserved grace
Discovered on the gauntlet of fire
You are whole you can inspire

More than enough always so
Only you were last to know
Rest easy let tears dry away
Slay dragons with a new sense of play

Have you been working head down without celebrating?
What harm pausing reflecting, refueling, reframing?
Benefit?

6 DANCING

Whatever comes stay in flow
Dance on currents as they blow
Hold fast visions of sacred ends
Stay open living navigate bends

Careful of rigid people and things
Hard edges stifle creative wings
Accept challenges of detours please
Allow their teaching learn with ease

Enraged by others needing control
Honor their illusion remain whole
Not about bossing or being right
It's peace of mind lying at night

Continue learning explore things
Allow fascinations engage beings
Honor directions from inside and out
Note chance meetings what they're about

Let nobility enter your conscious state
Don't worry much it's never late
Enjoy the simple expect great ends
Joy of communion many great friends

Treasure blessings bestowed on you
Love everyone despite what they do
Laugh at yourself when too serious
Enjoy ecstasy's flight unknown mysterious

Have places in your thinking become rigid with belief systems impacting your capacity to learn? Is your thinking getting in the way of growth?

7 FREEDOM

What holds you a boss a spouse
Job or family making you grouse
Life changes complaints quiet
Exercise a healthy diet

Make that happen blink of an eye
Gone self-pity reasons to cry
We hold keys of our capture
Inside a pathway to rapture

No manual parents can share
Discover self when you can't bear
No need to run or hide
Change all thoughts that bind

External movement won't get you there
Shift self-talk inside from fear
How you see what's served to you
Choose perspective gleeful or blue

Longing deprives you of sleep
Inside a need to weep
Lifetimes to cleanse your soul
Do it before growing old

World your oyster heaven here
No need escape nothing to fear
Jail a construct of your mind
Change thought forms leave prison behind

No need to wait to be set free
Today you've earned your degree
Listen to the voice of heart
Stay awake for your new start

Are the prisons you create based on reality or perceived truth?
Is there an affirming alternative?

8 FRESH

Complacent set in your way
Acting on habits day to day
Doing today what you did before
Being stops you are no more

Living with only routine things
Don't notice when a bell rings
Being busy with each chore
No room for so much more

Look for sparks saying alive
Things making you thrive
For newness in your life
Arts inventions your midwife

Want to birth new creation
Old no longer provides elation
Want to feel sense of pride
Honor depth buried inside

Living without vision
Of your sacred yards precision
When complacency yields strife
Time to reinvent your life

Has life become complacent with mindless habitual routines?
How can you create excitement beyond automatic behavior?

9 FAITH

Life is learning
Follow your yearning
Enable your rebirth
To reveal your deep worth

Longing peace to minimize loss
Stay away from destructive remorse
Don't lose childlike play
Rearrange things every day

Achievement income drives our world
We need solace from the mindless swirl
Changes come fast and deep
Changes too hamper sleep

Gravitate to what calms emotion
Belonging on a world in motion
Myth of control knowing what's so
Again and again always letting go

Emerge from a chrysalis state
See the world on a clean plate
Sorry there is no big plan
Let life reveal what it can

Take the steps that serve you well
Find the sanity where you dwell
To serve others for the long haul
Take care of yourself and stand tall

How do you maintain equanimity?
What throws you off and what keeps you on track?

10 POISED

Peace inside abiding
Grounded no more hiding
No longing let presence prevail
Use learning from life travail

Quiet silence fills heart brain
Deportment's even free of pain
No ego to be stroked and fed
Peace in body no chattering head

Joy in giving not getting gifts
Learning from your many rifts
Strong essence a struggler's find
Firmly implanted in the mind

Blessings in your divine dream
Time to honor powers supreme
Tools and vehicle on your ride
Accept proof god's at your side

You have all you need
No need to succumb to greed
Your giving clearly inspires
Satisfies all your desires

Do you appreciate good fortune and can you distribute your gift?
What's left to clear away?

11 MASTER-PLAN

Come serve a larger plan
Soldier of a marvelous clan
What's tomorrow for god to say
I'm servant I sit and pray

What she says I'll do her bidding
Honor my assignment that's fitting
Letting go of yesterday's plan
Trip worth taking shed all you can

Fill what's missing a pure hearts play
Engage the seriousness fill the day
Meditate quiet peaceful your presence
Letting go chatter serene your essence

Never give yourself away
Your power demands it's say
Inner wisdom funds this fight
Cleansing tears navigate dark night

In the end return to source
Angel status no remorse
You're part of bigger things
Take a breath flap your wings

Can you feel something bigger than you with a specific purpose?
How does that empower you?

12 REFRAMING

Periodically life asks all
Can you grow without a fall
Feeling trapped in chains
Let go after growing pains

Not external causing fears
Ego's construct locks our gears
Tension friction causing griefs
Dissonant self-concepts beliefs

War rages inside colored red
Then blue waters cool your head
Silent siting brings peace home
New habits of mind develop alone

Dear ones see and advise
We take it in if we're wise
Heed the voices begging attention
Expand to a new dimension

When twisted pulled by head and feet
Quiet old voices they'll defeat
Construct context to hold new you
Grow without the bitter blue

Embrace the gift of consciousness
A tool for your happiness
Lessons learned on earth plane
Add value please do not complain

How can you best leverage learning to let go of old belief systems?
When did you last consciously reframe something?

13 PATHFINDERS

For some easy finding their path
Traveling the cut of ordinary swath
Accept the standard of others direction
Rarely questions thoughts reflection

For many this works fine
Take care dear ones toe a line
Others' restless mind won't shut down
Life is searching unexamined ground

Can't stop seeking where few dare go
Unyielding exploring follow the flow
Cost measured in sleepless nights
Flights sometimes cost them their lives

Always question status quo
Foster innovation help others grow
Wake up calls for those asleep
Embracing soul it's all you keep

Awaken to power within
Don't listen to voices saying cannot win
Live experience the you emerging
Courageously mark ceaseless purging

Have you chosen a path worn by others?
Are you satisfied or are their course corrections you want to make?

14 BEATIFIC

Swirls encircle a troubled mind
Centered after all's left behind
Manic baffling makes you shout
Feeling good not what life's about

Eye in needle center of storm
Fire of life keeps you warm
Beneath action in buried mist
Peace transcends analysis

Burning glow serves sustains
That salve melts stings of pelting rains
Perspective when frayed and worn
Abiding laughter friendship in storm

Holy sacred inside profane
Force fields guide honors pain
Power enshrouds essential you
Centered kingdom where you rule

Seeking state of quiet inside
Stillness feeds cells their pride
In the center all worth is born
Holy beatific smile the norm

How do you get to the comfort and silent center of beingness?
What enables access and what does it generate?

15 NATURE

Heavenliness of nature's serenity
Pristine without industrialized humanity
Joyful perfection unfettered landscape
Shimmering waters leave you agape

Birds flying softly wind in air
Gold early sunlight crows' noises near
Sweet smelling flowers surrendering scent
White clouds blue sky another world sent

Respite of forest cool moss on trees
Mystery of quiet buzzing of bees
Roaring of ocean crashing of waves
Horizons' sunsets deserving of raves

In a hasty march through life
No time for inspiring sights
In stressed states forget to turn
Needing release from relentless churn

Remember to know what awaits you
Whenever weary or feeling blue
Nature's perfection holds gifts in store
Take time appreciate abundance galore

*Have you recently taken time to experience the beauty and comfort of nature?
What did that do for you?*

16 RESOLUTION

For getting to the other side
Let go old frames and pride
Move from gripped in fright
To new ground with delight

Mastery swaddled in your dream
From your triggers to serene
What was holding you in chains
No longer binds let go of pains

Conflict arises as we seek
Out there engaged testing meek
Yield power invest in others might
Then justify why we're right

Resolution provides peace
Wheels stop spinning let go release
Not when convincing yourself
It's the fault of someone else

Resolutions' about letting go
Choose to forgive time to grow
Understand perspectives they bring
Celebrate allow hearts to sing

They did not have you gripped by fears
Your constructs caused grinding gears
Perceiving from a new place
Your reward emergent grace

Have you resolved a disagreement by shifting perspective?
What was difficult to let go and was it worth it?

17 ART

Display fruit of labors
All sizes tastes flavors
Art shows where we've been
Evidence life more than whim

Shake shudder being born
Birthing leaves you torn
Reflect what's buried inside
Inside out no simple ride

Display what lives within
Takes courage and discipline
Open to critiquing minds
Comments at times unkind

Not afraid any longer
Bearing soul gets you stronger
Whatever they say and see
Not you likely thee

Personal art is holy spirit
Emerges with purity in it
Express your sweet being
Light what you are seeing

Continue in time space
No diverting from your pace
Let gifts unfold your way
Art reflects gods' holy play

How do you share observations and wisdom?
Does self-expression quiet fears and provide courage?

18 ATTENTION

Fear a teacher with much to give
Helps instruct how to live
Fearless get burned or worse
Know the difference or suffer the curse

Move without a sense of risk
Catastrophe in an instant brisk
Distraction without mindful gaze
Bereavement in unknown ways

Lose a finger lose an arm
Lose a loved one life-long harm
Lose a fortune position fame
Thoughtless lose their good name

To prevent calamities
Mindless brings you to knees
It is simple stay alert
Heed cautious voices sensing hurt

When you do a deed
Always follow warnings heed
Concerned voices always near
Trust lessons of healthy fear

Careful bravados joy ride
Honor warnings with mindful pride
Easy to always listen deep
Savor blessings never be sleep

What was the cost when you ignored a voice of fear?
What are you ignoring today?

19 COOPERATION

At a plateau in human evolution
Next rung demands a revolution
Got us here won't get us there
Shortcomings too much to bear

We keep exploiting corrupting
Continual ecology disrupting
Need balance thoughtful direction
Time for mindful course correction

Humans generated great invention
Amidst conquest civility pretension
Taming beasts mastering earth
Inventing machines was our worth

Harnessing time mastering space
Enslaving others our disgrace
Building means of mass destruction
Now it's time to stop construction

Time to conquer inner space
Or destroy the human race
Come together deep dialogues
Connection can heal wrongs

Moving forward in your life
Conscious choices as midwife
Commune with those in your space
Cooperation as your grace

Do you consider the earth and others when making resource choices?
Is cooperation an important value?

20 SELFLESSNESS

Lucky among us know about love
Honoring caring cooing a dove
Behind longing a desire for free
Of egos binding me me me me

Let go and let yourself burn away
Real love uplifts every day
Not about what you get for self
Shift the focus to someone else

Motherhood essence of birth
Caring for others provides more worth
When life shifts to other from you
Essential freedom turns off the blue

Observing with eyes ears heart
Seeing needs becomes your new art
Getting to giving shift is profound
Union communion on enduring ground

Understand where they come from
More than gold give platinum
In giving discover you don't need much
Caretaking satisfies way more than stuff

How do you feel when taking care of others?
What does it cost and what are the rewards?

21 INTEGRATED

Your space clear clean
Movements gracious actions lean
Illusions gone away
Polished excited new sense of play

Ground aerated feeling shined
Gone the shackles ties that bind
Circuitous route to arrive
Potential of a life that thrives

How why logic not yet revealed
Plaguing wounds somehow healed
Only duty be yourself
Why be anyone else

Stranger than fiction too
An integration with grounding true
No jerky movements in the air
At one with surroundings all are here

All's transparent now you know
All's revealed that helped you grow
Only next beyond this grace
Deliver gifts to the human race

What gifts do you bring and how do you deliver?
Can you provide leverage to gift to more people?

22 JOINING

Holds us together defines who we are
Without others do not go far
Part of design at the core
Alone limits in tandem we soar

Social beings need company of others
Working with sisters and brothers
Isolated we grow cold and quiet
Human engagement an essential diet

Withdraw and live alone
Lose touch with self and home
Others enliven draw out define
Reveal essence help us shine

Between us find the spark of life
Like egg and sperm husband wife
Energy emerges in hearts connecting
Missing in separations' defecting

Doing does not define who you are
Who you do with says who you are
Look for connections places to plug in
Joining with others provides powerful kin

Why does being with favorite others make you want more?
What sparks are created and what's produced?

23 SU WEN*

Possessing a unique pace
All together style and grace
After struggle pain
Humpty dumpty together again

Can't breathe gasp for air
Struggling for the there their
In throes grasping for life
Steep journey you the midwife

Passing through a needles eye
Fills you with awe and sigh
Though guides search with you
Only you can heal the blue

Invest in discovering self
Not measured by anyone else
Journey takes what it takes
Along the way a few outbreaks

Sure it will never fit
Pain and struggle want to quit
Glowing alive feeling pink
All together aligns in a wink

Keen eyes on the search
As you find a new perch
Wondering how and when
Stars align a su wen

How does a lack of integration detract from life?
What steps can you take to feel a sense of grace?

In acupuncture a single needle treatment
creating alignment and health

24 CIRCLES

Going forth seeking truth
Conquer mountains expend youth
Joyous giving all away
Discovering what makes a day

Scorching deserts freezing caves
Search for answers talk to graves
Where dwells wisdom profound
In the air underground

After exhausted searching longing
Finding little no belonging
In innocence and naivety
Know we knew with simplicity

Finally after many years
Joyous laughter howling tears
Full circle know what you want
Uncovering your sacred heart

Fortunes friendships lessons found
Journey of circles takes you round
The grounding place of long ago
Home hearth wisdom now you know

What are simple things you knew you would like to know again?
What can you share with young people about your journey?

25 STUFF

I wait delivery certain
For my stuff sofa chest curtain
Stuff I've been longing for
Suddenly through my door

Material things arrive
Candles dishes help me thrive
Sweaters shoes coats galore
Been without can't wait more

Amazing things become needs
Coveted possessions driving deeds
Suddenly don't need much
Perspective wisdom and such

Things don't respond relate warm
Cannot comfort buffer a storm
New shiny quickly get dull
Can't engage without pull

Reflect on what sustains
Possessions never maintain
People populate fill your life
Treasured gems your midwife

What are the most valued treasures you've invested in?
How have priorities around relationships developed and changed?

26 VERGES

Life sends us places
Conundrums tensions faces
Situations to mull over
Anxiety like clover

Long peace in life and work
Persist in not being a jerk
Sitting broiling stewing bubbling
Pouring salt on wounds troubling

Many choose to sit and stew
Others search for what's new
Standing alone on their track
See from places not so black

Whatever happens to you
Why hold stress too
Search a tack to take
When contribution to make

Tension a positive force
Pulls you back to central source
Notice how life emerges
Guiding you thru powerful verges

Is there dissonance in your life between standards and actions?
Can you hold tension as creative productive energy?

27 SMILES

Ordinary smile and grin
Tickling parts generate whim
Thoughts intersect disparate places
Disjointed connections laughing graces

Sometimes clear realization
Wry smiles reflect elation
Friendly greetings welcome here
At ease opens ear to ear

Smiles express feelings inside
Sharing warmth relating pride
Create connection and exchange
Immediate bonding is the change

Demonstrate a happy heart
Body shares a joyous start
Growing older closer to core
Approaching god wanting more

Spontaneous grins say all's OK
Saying words you cannot convey
Generously giving sweetest smiles
Crosses chasms bridging miles

Goes where mind cannot go
Connecting you are not alone
Showering nectar from above
Sacred gift shares purest love

Who have you smiled at today, when they smiled back what did you feel?
What might more smiling bring?

28 SEARCHING

Everywhere answers lie
Caves seas in mind's eye
Answers in sacred text
New plateau what is next

Consult sages beseech oracles
For answers to what is and was
Plan next steps on your quest
Consult rabbi priest who's best

Search seek to and fro
Back to mirror time to grow
Other's wisdom clear and true
Responsibility always you

No fear you have all you need
Still voice inside listen heed
When searching reaches end
Only lie with your best friend

Marching to your destiny
Searching is where you're free
Journey satisfies in life
Seeking awakens appetite

What searching informs your destiny?
Who are allies and who resists?
What happens when you stop seeking?

29 SUBLIME

Internal voices silent serene
Life a lovely liquified dream
Quiet clear no fretting fuss
They all part of your us

Everyone has essentials in hand
Life idyllic though rarely bland
Education arts health housing too
Needs taken care of for you

Political borders erased
No matter ethnicity religion or race
What we know gives assurance to all
Whatever dreams follow their call

Compassion ends criminality
Wisdom releases mania finally
Systems in place serving needs
Life's reason art and good deeds

All things you worry about
Crimes making you scream and shout
People you fear in an uneasy way
Given a gift their sense of play

Can this be done in your life or mine
Giving up power for a world sublime
We have more than each of us needs
Technology education whatever feeds

Not idle dreaming lets make a plan
Starts with each woman and man
Cherish the vision possibility worth
Heaven now right here on earth

Do we have enough?
Do we have a resource or distribution challenge?

30 BLESSINGS

Each day count blessings dear
Embrace friends keep them near
Joy of living smiles on faces
Cherished ones sacred spaces

Pleasure in connections to others
Beaming at sisters brothers
Shaking laughter smell of perfume
Greetings on entering a room

Touch of another when down
Warm hugs dissolve a frown
Exciting friend you've not seen
Eating favorite ice cream

Grilled steak red wine
Stadium cheers game on the line
Millions of stars twinkles to count
Joys outshine a bank account

End of day nothing new
Dance of dog greeting you
Kiss of a lover mouth open deep
Sharing breath drift off to sleep

What blessings can you appreciate and count today?
Can you see your cup running over?

May

1 ABUNDANCE

Living tests inner strength
For abundance joy radiance
Nothing bad in material wealth
For many prosperity's health

Suffering poverty starvation
An ethos of purification
Current era a great test
Is materialism best

In times of great wealth
Few value a holy self
Easy being righteous and such
Without any sense of too much

Giving your excess away
Sharing part of your pay
Daily measure what you gave
Philanthropy not what you save

Stay centered right and true
Earn grow provide too
In a needed next evolution
All riches perhaps the solution

*How do you think about possessions and acquisitions - what do material
things provide and not?*
How might you change your relationship to things?

2 FRIENDSHIP

Dear friends don't need a mirror
They're object you're a giver
Hold heal stretch reveal
Keep on course sturdy keel

What they provide you can't assess
In money gold or success
Allow who you are
Needed they come far

Love accept what you do and say
Disagree respect anyway
Gentle cajoling keeps you on toes
See misgivings when you're no rose

Presence comforts is transparent
When required they're a parent
Come in all sizes shapes colors
Add to family sisters brothers

Chill anxiety lower hypertension
Help you choose new direction
In the end ready to go
Bless passing their love aglow

Honored by riches friends hold
Don't be shy tell them they're gold
Acknowledge them and their gift
Let them know they're your lift

Keep cherish all they do
Kiss tell them you need their purview
Set you afire like a shining star
Friends enable who you are

Who do you count as friends and do they know their mean?
How can you honor and acknowledge them?

3 ENGAGEMENT

No greater excitement than the start
New job team project love work of art
Air of expectancy crackles alive
Creativity buzzing no need to strive

Joy infuses all you do
Life has focus purpose renewed
Brain feels like sunspots exploding
Bubbling always no signs of imploding

Lift off arrives grounding traction
Engagement deepens purposeful action
Awareness of mission you're engaging
Cellular structure rearranging

Presence engages without confusion
Experience satisfying communion
Joy of grace kiln like intensity
Curbs procrastination self-doubt propensity

Suggest developing the habit
If routine enslaves quick as jackrabbit
Let freshness excite creative spirit
Whatever the prize you can win it

Recall projects that energized and engaged at the beginning?
What contributed to lessening attention and what helped you stay engaged?

4 FUTURE

Design tomorrow for yourself
Assess terrain choose off the shelf
Unique quality as animals
Look front back discern will be was

Power residing birthright we share
Use this might for goodness and dare
Planet we inhabit needs strong intention
Billion daily need modeling direction

Time ripe crisis calls concentrate
Given the at stake no time to wait
Look at your life what can you do
Harness intent change stewing brew

In a complex world ambiguous too
Deciding what's next takes me and you
Align plans agree on joint vision
Do it now no indecision

Tomorrow in your minds eye
Not what you borrow what you tithe
Not being a taker provides some glee
Giving awakens best in you and me

What are you contributing today for the future?
How can you share a larger goal and what's at stake?

5 AWAKENING

Suddenly your slate is clean
Gone disappeared was a bad dream
For years held you in chains
Let go released no longer remains

Joy you relish waits for you
This moment embrace the new
Cherish the presence you yearned
A blessings that you have earned

Gone the demons chattering mind
The insane all left behind
Arisen awakened in love
Blessed by gods from above

Royal inheritance that's you is real
Bearing you carry let it reveal
Step into now to quench your thirst
No longer second you are now first

All your good wishes coming true
Gift of your giving comes back to you
No need for striving you're already done
Honor the moment you've just begun

Are you pleased where you are or do you have more ground to cover
this lifetime?
Can you enjoy the journey?

6 ALIVE

Privilege to be alive in a body
Feeling joyful tearful hardy
Endowed with magical tools and gifts
For navigating shifts upon shifts

Always a companion never alone
Familiar knowing who is home
Heartening comfort warming sincere
Always present year after year

Whatever fate or serendipity brings
Your vehicle serves as wings
Processors Intel longs for
Robotics with intelligence galore

Complex sentience powerful emotion
The presence of sacred devotion
Independence dependence interdependence too
Reinvention part of our stew

Honor your body it is your friend
Serving needs to the end
Cherish it with gratitude treat it well
Your magic carpet never will tell

Do you acknowledge and appreciate your physical body?
What might you change about caring for this part of yourself?

7 GYROSCOPE

Recover naturally
Avoid toxicity
Mind body regeneration efficient
Assess needs where deficient

Elegantly choose direction
Best path to perfection
Powerful keystone genius heart
Voice a sense of art

Focus on words deep within
Hear messages never whim
They set a guiding course
Follow to prevent remorse

Your wisdom superb gyroscope
Supercomputer your best hope
Access source get quiet and still
Ask questions beyond will

In recovery trust inner voices
Ignore chatter abide hearts choices
Delivery from demons inside
Healing certain enjoy the glide

Have you listened to inner guidance for what needs healing?
How do you get out of the way and let the wisdom guide?

8 GOD/LOVE

How do you know you've met god
Hear a welcome with knowing nod
Sense security warmth within
Compassionate heart knowing grin

Wander earth in peaceful delight
Sleep sweetly through the night
All well loved ones on a path
No harboring anger or wrath

Longing for peace on earth
Feeling full without girth
Life work fills a noble mission
Blessings of selfless vision

Dear ones draw forth compassion
Fight injustice with great passion
A circle of love in your life
Relationships flow without strife

No fear of death to come
Know where power is from
Understand what's written above
Blessed to know god is only love

What's the thinking behind your responses?
Do you see needed inner and outer work?

9 ORIGINS

Coming together people in places
Surrounded by familiar faces
Less common today as we roam
So remember place you call home

World fixated on progress growth
Be mindful of your loyalty oath
Not about what you give them
A gift to remembering when

Honoring where you came from
Learned through lenses of someone
Cherish past look to tomorrow
In the present minimize sorrow

Timeless truth without doubt
We get smart finding out
Thank honor the part they play
Their presence showed a way

Loving learning living such
Contributing to you so much
Without them not you or me
From there learned how to be thee

Who do you stay in touch with to keep you grounded?
What do connections provide and who do you want more time with?

10 HEALTH

What is health for you or me
Vantage point a different see
Each has standards to find
Embedded in a fertile mind

Measure for each not the same
Answers have a different name
For all bottom line
What makes you feel fine

Some go early live at both ends
Longevity not their friends
Some around forever it seems
Satisfied keep opening dreams

Others mark journey of life
Home hearth for them is nice
What's sure for you and me
Occupy different reality

Abusing the body takes years
Others suffer personal tears
Health mindset attitude perspective
Discern each prescribed directive

Listen to your heart develop will
Freedom's call dictates your fill
Find many friends on the trail
When your time ends alone you sail

How do you define your state of health and are you healthy?
What do you need to do more or less of to be healthy?

11 STRENGTH

Pulls you to new heights
Pushes movement despite freights
Fosters expansion to the brink
Take us places would not think

Holds us together through rain
Reminder of essential salving pain
Stronger than steel roots piercing rock
Little attention to weather or clock

Constant carrying us through
Manifesting soul makes sure we do
We came for task and mission
Living that without indecision

Strength and center of soul and genes
Guiding unfolding through our screams
Possess free will to do as we choose
When exercised sometimes we lose

Further faster go with flow
Listen soft voices buried below
Follow the wisdom honor your heart
Let them design you like elegant art

Weathering storms of pain
Quiet messages better than brain
Grail not to fight but to be in flow
Perfect wisdom strength to let go

What is the voice you trust, where does it come from and what does it reflect?
Do you access and follow it consistently?

12 SUFFERING

Searing heartbreak much to teach
Transmute burning larger reach
White heat suffering anguish pains
Tempers character what remains

Crowning compassion is your prize
In discomfort hearts grow wise
Screams and anguish quiet cease
Peace is left after release

Easy choice spare the pain
Sweet diversions hide the rain
Avoid discomfort growing art
Deflection insulates knowing heart

Your pathway a road to select
Cultivates a will erect
Journey offered not for weak
Highway there for those who seek

Honorable suffering grows the self
Rewards your life not someone else
Value courage required to persist
Strength transcends urge to resist

Know the beauty of spirit pure
Relish blessings of every door
Rest peaceful quiet know the gift
Freedom grace in ashes you sift

In what ways has suffering enhanced your learning?
Would you be the same without the pain?

13 GRACE

Quiet silence breathing clean
Vibration of a slow motion dream
Dancing brain on crow's nest perch
At last ceased your incessant search

Warring factions strangely serene
Birdsong prevails a bucolic scene
Dear ones happy pointed true north
Longing filled wellbeing warmth

Night sky star full days blue sunshine
Filling heavens pleasing sublime
Restless abandon a thoughtless plight
Vanished leaving pure delight

Centered presence of pure breath
Nirvana crowned you with happiness
New understanding how life can fit
In this precious moment do not resist

Step into this deserving grace
Moment to moment this your new place
One of the blessed embracing the new
Your noise peeled away arrived at true

What has been the presence of grace like in your life,
how long did it last and how did you know it arrived?
What prevents knowing that more often?

14 ENERGY

Carries you toward
Compels without reward
Vision for future
In the distance to nurture

Clear what to manifest
Passion yields the best
Spark of creation deep in being
Crystal white light no one seeing

Laser point infecting cells
Fire ringing all your bells
Internal alarm summons musters
Once alive filibusters

Call it love electricity
Aliveness eccentricity
Call it essence call it spirit
Call it god purely live it

When quiet meditating
What's in you vibrating
Unleash power living inside
Focus aim watch it thrive

What vision drives and expresses your purpose?
What would you like to leave as contribution and legacy?

15 JOYOUS

What a journey and joy
Drink in laughter say oh boy
Life for living cavort with friends
Glowing light supply never ends

Wellspring smiles from your heart
Keep the grin a form of art
Intention to affirm life
The way to overcome strife

Abundant source propping wings
Unlimited for all manner of things
Essence of giggles eau de warm glances
Many dance steps informing prances

Richest hugs eyes that contact
Connection of minds keeps you on track
Beauty of nature surrounds all the time
When words fail pantomime

Sunsets daily say goodnight to flowers
Dogs wagging tails mark many hours
Take some time notice these presents
Filling life with the gift of presence

*What makes your life joyous, lifts spirits makes you laugh and
engages enthusiasm?*
What do you do when you need a lift?

16 ENGAGED

Joy of deeply felt traction
Engaged by passion driven to action
Striving something bigger than you
Deeply committed heart is true

Not about money fame recognition
Not about you about mission
Something noble can't do alone
Something grabs deep in the bone

Pulling you toward a vision a dream
Guiding actions creating a scheme
Longing heart satisfied filled
No pining motivated willed

Compelling what you do each day
A purpose with you lighting the way
Buzzing inside comes from source
If loved ones can't abide they divorce

Driven by mission and urgency
Clear conviction makes you free
Righteous abandon lightening spark
Your shining makes light of dark

How engaged are you with current work and a mission?
Is your daily work aligned with a purposeful mission?

17 SELF-ASSURANCE

Ready to let yourself be known
Sharing from deep in your bone
No hiding from fear of put down
Share your wisdom travel to town

Trust inner wisdom honor your truths
Smile at rejection mentor many youths
Define ambition on your terms
Fight the battles sharing your words

Let go illusions others hold dear
Bring to each day best of good cheer
Make sure loved ones at your side
Keep pace on their own magical ride

Trust faith is there with you
Comforting losses to carry all through
When not sure what to do
Honor the cloudy to all be true

Say yes to all above
Gods will honor your sacred love
Hold this present each day
Foster wisdom and learn to play

Not what you own on earth
Not an identity or measure of worth
Share openly nod and wink
Treasure deepest thoughts that you think

Are lessons you deliver an extension of yourself or do you hold back?
How can you get beyond resistance?

18 CONTRIBUTION

This moment whatever your place
Opportunity to dance in the human race
A joy in this era has been revealing
People are craving sacred healing

Think of your genius and gifts
How to partake in healing rifts
We need blessings so share them all
Joyously engage the celebratory ball

Midst of savagery chaos fear
Chance to shine beckons here
World loves a player answer your call
No hording genius be generous to all

Recite poetry sing organize educate
No sitting or waiting embrace gyrate
Brothers sisters all need your gifts
Share to foster their essential shifts

Don't hesitate waiting for perfect
Don't hide and say you are not worth it
Get beyond frozen safe in your fear
Time for action be brave and sincere

What gifts have you been hiding?
Who would benefit from your sharing hidden gifts?

19 DISCOVERY

In unions boundaries define
Engage to see the line
Tightly bonded to someone else
Teaches and discovers self

Driven by fear not play
Get close to others run away
Fear losing self and identity
Drama pushes you and me

Want to fully explore
Merge with others be reborn
Boundaries keep you apart
Remember share a joyous heart

Faith courage discovery of you
Through life entwine others too
Survive unions in which you melt
Bounce back discover a new self

Tension forces you to express
Uniqueness making you yourself
Present if you remain intact
Do not bow to another's act

Listen speak as you emerge
Notice birthing power surge
Counter-intuitive to what you know
Own your essence engage and grow

Have you learned about yourself engaged with others?
Given we discover ourselves in relationship who do you chose to be with
and how do they support self-discovery?

20 ENGAGEMENT

Key to wisdom and happiness
Engagement leads to success
Let life define you not you defining it
Imposing ego may lead you to a pit

Interaction defines who you are
Without feedback can't go very far
Choose a fertile canvas and play
Informed by what others say

Context for growth learning
Let inner voices speak their yearning
Let experience provide teaching
Aware of aims you're reaching

In professional and personal spheres
Never forget only so many years
What you want to leave behind
Pursue with passion don't live blind

Find folks you love be open real
Give all away nothing to steal
Treat them as they want to be treated
Don't sit back even when depleted

Think in grand terms about legacy
Want for others what sets them free
Be heard your voice strong and clear
Your whole self year after year

What do you do for others without thinking about it?
If you designed your life around giving that to others what might it look like?

21 GODHEAD

What is peace tranquility
Nectar joy stability
Gift it carries gives so much
Not in doing achievement or such

It's the glue force power
Holding you each moment hour
Filling space of the void
Present even when annoyed

It is sea sky ground and air
What is empty filled with care
When things get in your way
Godhead presence saves the day

Never alone or off course
Blessing through all remorse
What you want it can see
Sweet gentle bird buzzing bee

Holds caresses each sacred soul
Tickles toes fills any hole
Lifts you to the brightest stars
Beyond restraints removes all bars

Life's a gift good being here
Be thankful and say a prayer
Rejoice celebrate privileged living
With gratitude always be giving

Do you relish joy, breathing, tasting, hugging, giving and loving dear ones?
What more could you want?

22 BEGINNING

Start with energy sparkles glows
Quickens thinking wakes up toes
Excites body tickles mind
Pulls you places leave self behind

Dawning visions let go fears
Breaking chains of many years
Reinvention possible now
Time for rebirth figure out how

Best part of starting new
Do no matter what was then true
No matter how stuck or the place
Power now to discover grace

No need to move body or stuff
Or travel on a car train or bus
Use a new mind set direction
Sense of purpose with intention

Step out of your own way
Let inner guidance navigate any fray
One day wake up you are there
Starting over despite old fear

How does it feel to began a project with clarity of purpose?
What do you want to begin today?

23 OPTIONS

Life serves choices you decide
Each fork impacts your glide
One way life sublime
Another tack struggle time

Always reap what you sow
Karma beyond mortal control
Youth ignore consequence
Without thinking comeuppance

Traveling mind your Ps and Qs
Conscious of lessons choices choose
Stinging outcomes hurt at the core
Reminding you must learn more

Vise of options clenches jaws
Blindly barrel or give yourself pause
Choose wisely for posterity's sake
What flows from decisions you make

Pain of others always dear
Haunts perspective in your ear
Selfish satisfies immediate thirst
Mindful of fallout avoids the worst

Your humanity sets you apart
Beyond instinct a compassionate heart
Add self-consciousness reflection too
Abstract thought a complex brew

Time for choosing now is here
Vote for life stay in fear
Best to be your highest self
As fear fades just be yourself

Do you think about what flows from action and its' impact on your and others' soul?

24 HEALING

Precious moment current time
Reveal yours I'll reveal mine
Reveling in other sharing our own
In exchange seeds are sown

Naked innocence was concealed
In sacred exchange both are healed
Journeying forward uncovering more
Deliverance assured find what it's for

Smiles laughter in cherished breath
Sublime exchange of tenderness
Warmth passing being to being
A dream state beneath seeing

Realize what's going on
Holy communion a new dawn
Smiling knowing on your face
Embody insides sharing grace

Mindful tender pure intention
Admittance to another dimension
Respect cherish honor bestowed
Bless the comfort traveling home

What was the feeling in a powerful encounter that transformed your life?
Would life be different if you missed that opportunity and what are you missing
right now?

25 ALIVE

Privilege being alive in a body
Feeling joyful tearful hearty
Navigating shifts upon shifts
With wonderful tools and gifts

Always company never alone
Familiar know how we're prone
Present available year after year
Heartfelt comfort warming sincere

What fate serves or stupidity brings
Our vehicle serves as our wings
Robotics with intelligence galore
Processors Intel longs for

Complex range of thinking emotion
Powerful sense of connection devotion
Independence dependence interdependence
Reinvention to maintain our relevance

Honor your vehicle it is a friend
Serves your needs to the end
Cherish thank treat it well
Magical ride that never will tell

Are you thankful for your physicality?
Have you been neglectful and what can you change about your self-care?

26 REJUVENATION

No matter how frazzled or spent
Nature is always a vent
Releasing tension curing what ails
Quietly digested recalibrates sails

Why this effect simple enough
Nature's purity embodies god's stuff
Each leaf perfect each fern and rock
No greater design on any block

Feeling empty chilled alone
Get out in nature sooth the moan
Feeling empty chilled alone
Nature's embrace guides you home

How can you experience the renewing power of nature today?
What's intoxicating about natural phenomenon?

27 LARGESS

Ready to realize tomorrow
Little you need to borrow
Come far moved quick
Concerns handled in the nick

Foundation solid true
Enough for me and you
Technology resources for all
Distribution prevents a fall

Unfortunate few grasp how excess
Creates an environmental mess
Power to conquer we have means
Better off in old blue jeans

Survival begs a compelling vision
No time for indecision
Worthwhile world for human beings
Home community food and dreams

More than enough for everyone's needs
Critical context fosters great deeds
Set minds on a noble quest
Enough for on our nest

What inspires a personal and societal future?
Do you need more material things or things of far greater value?

28 LOVE

Warm soft feeling in you
Alongside as you do
Replacing anxiety filling space
Joyous laughter call it grace

Lifts horizons wakens essence
All the time animating presence
It's inside not out there
Filling you bringing cheer

Longing a driver of many years
Finally quiet tears disappeared
On arrival yearning ceased
Suddenly you are released

In rebirthing old self died
Radical shift new sense of pride
Instead of not enough
Helping smooth others stuff

Difference a lifetime makes
Giving not one who takes
Days filled with divine bliss
Sweetest laughter spark of kiss

When were you infused with love as a presence more than the product of
a relationship?
What sensation do you access and proudly own?

29 SMALLTALK

Many times you spent a year
Someone's hour filled your ear
Dribble drabble of their life
Minutia of mundane strife

If you had a recording tape
Made them listen no escape
Did they think of the impact
Their stories show lack of tact

Nice if all had a filter
Speech had a content sniffer
We would know if anecdotes
Mean that much to other folks

Now I've risked being profound
Think I'll have a turn around
Content not as important
As presence and comportment

What's recalled after contact
More than the words impact
Smiles warm reception eyes connect
Evoke something to reflect

Comfort sensed in other's presence
Authenticity revealed their essence
After spending a slice of time
Is the experience peace of mind

What makes you want more connection with someone?
Do you use the same metric evaluating your impact on others?

30 SEEKING

Incomplete at birth
Our quest on earth
No certainty so
Search so you grow

Searching for a vision clear
Seekers work is in their ear
Long for moments still
No concern you can't fill

Where's your place on this rock
Want more time on the clock
Partners' presence bolsters will
Missing part they might fill

On this journey called life
Suffering amidst all strife
Not for the timid weak or slow
It's the strong making a go

In the middle of this pain
Amid angst is there gain
You've come through many traps
Keep searching for your synapse

Soon likely you will find
Salve to sooth your raging mind
In the end you will know
Who it was that loved you so

What path have you been traveling and what's missing?
How do you find strength when depleted and what provides solace?

31 PROMISES

What drives guides directs
Sets intention if down resurrects
Foundation of projects we choose
Uplifts spirits subsumes bad news

Much bigger than small selves
Eternal pulls us off our shelves
Commitments promises to others
Link in a chain of sisters brothers

Actions reflect our stance
Choosing steps of a personal dance
Widening circles expanding reach
Opens the joy to learn and teach

Capacity expands results multiply
Joining others stretches our sky
What we owe they expect
Entitled to promises kept

What this says as you reflect
Know your promises at peril neglect
Others rely on what you say you'll do
Honor self-worth to others be true

How does keeping promises impact reputation and integrity?
Do you renegotiate before promised performance is due or deliver when you get
to it?

June

1 LOVING

Generates energy sets you free
Provides power unleashes your me
Supporting presence opens mind
Launches a way can't be left behind

Wakes you to power within
Points a direction always a win
Clarifies vision focuses goals
Creates fail-safe making you whole

Quiets fears engages passion
Removes resistance generates compassion
Opens hearts slows chattering mind
Feeds deepest hunger while being kind

Sustains you through laughter and tears
Walks beside for many years
Provides comfort when enraged
Reengages when estranged

Can you sense all the above
Warm peaceful quality of love
A lovely freedom on this earth
Power of loving fills you with worth

What's the quality of love you give and receive?
How can you improve the love in your life you give to yourself?

2 PERSEVERANCE

Clarity knows a path is correct
Genius learns from pointed criticism
Magic befriends detractors
Grounded stands firmly whatever comes
Faith honors inner guidance in uncertainty
Compassion cares for others when you have little
Balance leaves more than it takes
Perseverance continues in the face of adversity
Endgame finds comfort in its skin and aspires

What do you think and feel about these aspirations?
How does your daily practice support them?

3 SMILING

Enlivening spirit evoking god
Emanating presence knowing nod
Rising from center overflowing delight
Capturing beauty a smiling sight

Sparkling spirit emerges from within
Emanating essence with a wide grin
Joy the blessing of being alive
Nothing to reach nothing to strive

Allow transformation darkness to light
No need for worry sunrise heals fright
About letting go of fog and mist
Step into the bubble of your sacred tryst

Wash away memories of yesterday's pain
Cleansing awakens rinsed by fresh rain
Allow divine union of you and grace
Beaming a smile covering your face

Sharing with others you are the seed
Vanishing envy replacing greed
Distributing manna showing the way
Birthing new dawn each wonderful day

What does it feel like when you're in the zone?
What contributed, how can you perpetuate?

4 APPRECIATION

Both beginning and an end
Life relentless at every bend
Surprise as we pretend command
Drawing cards can't predict the hand

Never expected to feel this depth
Profound emotion draining strength
Change accepting sense of fate
Learning perspective value of mate

You honored this young man
Cavalierly dismissed your plan
Realize all I did not see
Unable to give more of me

Tell myself I'll be OK
Through trauma return to everyday
In living lessons become
At the bone know the world from

A new place on sacred earth
Broader vista tolerance mirth
Loved you dear one more than you know
Connected forever souls dance so

When did you see in hindsight realizing something you were blind to?
What lessons did you take and are you now more awake, conscious, mindful?

5 INSPIRATION

Enduring beauty a form of art
Memories in a lingering heart
Stirring feelings passions rise
Impressions on a body mind

Create a container for the above
Seeing objects demanding love
Draw attention engage notice
Beautiful demands your focus

Essential purity of design
Integrated composition noble mind
Halting appearance seductive will
Perfect stature provides a chill

Poetry painting sculpture dance
Classical music south of France
Rap Beethoven Wolfgang Puck
Creative genius a bit of luck

Exciting presence you want home
Captured so it will not roam
A moving form lifting spirits
Transcendence gifting many minutes

Do you have beautiful things around to appreciate?
Why do value about them?

6 RECOGNITION

Not worked for nice if received
When it happens feel relieved
Spend life on a mission
Dreams guided by vision

Working toward a goal each day
Trying this that having your say
Progress measured by traction
Seeing others joining action

Others know what you're doing
Realize what you're brewing
They engage with your vision
Recognizing work and mission

Now no time to collapse
No falling ego relapse
Back slapping no effect on head
Not about you getting others fed

You the channel you the steward
Moving the vision forward through it
Remain vigilant through elation
Key is always your vibration

What is your personal mission, what draws you too it?
How will the world be different because you were here?

7 HEARTSONG

Deeply grateful can't ask more
Blessed this life abundance galore
Friendships lovers many fans
Not much saying sans

Joyous beginnings deep rich ends
Though the journey gave me bends
Searching lessons inquiries deep
Learning curve at times steep

Many teachers stand on shoulders
Answers from many wiser olders
Mentors many forms and faces
Beautiful their sharing graces

Knowing's not as fun as not
Emerging gifts you can't plot
Standing silence sitting dark
Waiting for a gift a spark

Learning patience in the core
Encouraging presence I came for
Take what's so as a gift
Correct translation not a rift

One step next reveals a path
The glow of lumens sacred bath
Breathe deep hear a call stay in grace
Focus attention sail time and space

Blessed abundance fills your cup
When thirsty service fills you up
Follow heart song let melody infuse
Rhythms inform honor lullaby blues

Seek ways of giving on your path
Generosity trumps buried wrath
Keep the covenant do your best
Allow stillness quiet peace rest

Accomplishment not who you are
Let light shine help get them far
Laugh let tears fall smile be wise
Let spirits grace paint scenes in eyes

In the end happiness to know
Gifts here to borrow tap the flow
Dissolve walls as you navigate
All's OK you've passed the gate

*What would be cause for celebrating yourself
and your life? Who knows how deserving you
are and would be part of the celebration?*

8 PLENTY

More than enough no need to worry
Have what you need no need to scurry
Food from the earth so many ways
Infants are born white light star gaze

No longer hunted by carnivores
When that occurs give them what fors
Scientific advancements magical minds
New things enabled miraculous finds

Most without struggle for basic needs
Feeding the hungry and doing good deeds
Why all the fighting and incessant war
Why the blindness to what we're here for

Many with power beauty sublime
No sense of owning what's yours or mine
Potential unlimited for all in need
Why the darkness with swords and greed

Nasty bad guys parade in white
Time to forsake be they left or right
Wolves at our tables in cloaks that conceal
Time to unmask time to reveal

Righteous speak with forked tongue truth
Time they were booted back to their youth
Food from the earth in so many ways
Infants are born white light star gaze

What daily miracles do you acknowledge?
Can you see more of what happens on earth as miraculous?

9 PATIENCE

Troubled by grasping and will
Exerting demands pushing to fill
Disregard others refuse to let go
Selfish wanting plaguing you so

Rather than accept and step into flow
Try to control thinking you know
Assume earth a human playground
Finally realize other species abound

Dare I suggest for those here now
Time to be bigger with a new vow
Let go of ego let go of will
Practice patience learn to be still

Accept life get out of your way
Surely take some time for play
What serves on a seeker's path
Conserve energy cut down wrath

Let go of what you think should be
Take care of business a way to be free
Honor true self the one deep inside
Filled with deep wisdom there you reside

When this that happens not about bliss
Satisfaction fleeting like a lover's kiss
Take nurture from patience choose let go
See up down process of your small ego

Step into easy let presence emerge
Forget abandon it will tax your nerve
In detachment hearts quietly sing
Love for the asking don't do anything

What can you learn from stillness and observing chattering mind body?
Can you make that presence part of your practice?

10 BEAUTY

Without within
An elated grin
Generated by what we see
Always a spark of glee

Most say eyes of beholder
Wiser as you get older
No doubt a mixture both
Look out and in for worth

Real beauty we seek
Peace contentment mind meek
Self-assured having command
Of your vehicle it's so grand

Not just physical no
Mental emotional so you grow
Ability to regulate self
Responsibility is great wealth

You are source and guide
Godhead on your side
Move forward grow new ways
Beauty creating blissful days

How do you define beauty?
When did you last create something beautiful?

11 BEAUTIFUL

Real beauty a lustrous scene
Natural no artificial sheen
Alive authenticity projected
Poised assured rarely dejected

Proud resolve path mission
Steadfast earnest no contrition
Telling truth no compromise
Pure as moon sundown sunrise

Cat like stealth feline
Scent of rose velvet wine
Clear vibration as a source
Rarely do you see remorse

Alluring always at center
Answers serve as mentor
Clear values wrong and right
If uncertain always insight

Pleasure to be with and observe
Not often losing nerve
Chronicle teaching wisdom shared
Lessons always make you glad

No need for seeking presence enough
Purity in bearing strong never tough
There to admire no need for yes
Being inspires you must confess

Not easily captured can't subdue
Drinks from its' well a magical brew
Honor the being notice the flow
Its' character helps you to grow

Don't try to be it model the essence
Take on the aura it's holy presence
Honor the freedom self-assured ways.
Beauty a beacon in a world of haze

Who and what do you consider beautiful?
Why?

12 FAMILY

Feeling whole safe needed rest
Relax let go all that's not best
Peaceful presence over you
No need search be in what's true

Warmth of being known
Freedom comfort you are home
Essential welcome context deep
Richest slumber needed sleep

Blessing bestowed on you
Enables what you're called to do
External glory from that ground
Your foundation so profound

Fortunate you received this gift
The beginning supports each shift
Potential glory reflected in you
Loving always seeing you through

Perspective and wisdom imparted
Values meaning compassion started
Gift of family a deep solid core
Supporting what you came for

Moving forward carving your path
The scythe of giving cuts a wide swath
Remember your source of strength
Ennobling values your great wealth

How has your context supported your journey?
What lessons were part of your foundation and what helped you
through adversity?

13 GRADUATION

Celebrate a passage of life
New plateau beyond strife
Not the first or the last
Engage graduations come fast

Time for reflection joy
You are no one's toy
For milestones not so real
Accomplishment hard to feel

Pause a moment drink it in
Achieved a deserved win
This one very big
Real adult lovely gig

Self-possession special feel
Center of your new real
Responsibility ups downs
Healing other's frowns

Honor moments mark time
New presence proud and fine
No small thing to pass this test
Soak it in with earnestness

When dear ones have cause for celebration do you honor them?
Who can you celebrate today?

14 ATTITUDE

Quality many desire
A reason to aspire
Consciousness in fashion
Catalyst igniting passion

Long for it in detail
Embrace it or you flail
Quality sustains and guides
Essential for a life that glides

Not who or what it's attitude
Cultivated mind beatitude
Perspective helps understand
Expectations when too grand

Miracles everyday
Kindness in the fray
Empathy time to attach
A great movie watch

Voices speaking quietly
Map and compass set you free
Smile hug don't run away
Here today not yesterday

What makes you happy?
What do you need to stop, continue and begin doing?

15 EXASPERATION

Where to go charge is low
Energy waning no place to go
Horizon looking bleak
Fear grips cannot speak

Alarm says wake up you say no
Nothing worth it so why go
Pennies can't pay the rent
Your get up got up and went

Look up clouds in the sky
Longing present cup is dry
Screams inside all so mean
Future vision a blank screen

Inside out want to cry
Loved ones no help though they try
Laughter smiles abandoned face
All worked for gone no trace

Place to turn within you
Each cell says I want to do
Primordial urge live from essence
Who you are contribute presence

How much focus is on your inner voice?
What happens when you do not pay attention to that wisdom?

16 REVELATION

Clarity quiets your soul
No more striving you are whole
Nothing missing no place to go
Stay present learn and grow

No false illusions residing
Confusion gone no more hiding
Frantic searching of history
Receding focus on me me me me

Lighthouse beckoned a last time
A path resplendent hues sublime
Within all your need
Earthly journey a good deed

A plateau sings to your heart
Validates the journey enables art
Prowess emerges as you ride
Assurance god is inside

Let revelations quiet your fear
Sacred wisdom always near
Time to share gifts you hold
Nurture wisdom as you grow old

Where are you with clarity, mission, legacy and achieving what you came for?
What do you still have to accomplish?

17 COMMUNION

Drinking others sweet essence
Nourishment basking in presence
Courage through humility's fear
Truly listening to really hear

Coming together souls on a path
Provides each a pure sacred bath
Cleansing spirits renewing soul
Restoring vitality once again whole

Sacred path to a place called home
Joyous truthful never alone
Speaking of missions and lofty things
Fuel of communion provided wings

Amazing grace across time and space
Assistance of a warm healing place
Connections deepened quickening arose
Laughter generated energy flows

Intelligence blended collective born
Capacity unfolding beyond the norm
Wisdom emerged with ease out of mist
That was the joy of our sweet noble tryst

Last time you were part of a creative community what did you receive, give and learn?

18 SOFTNESS

Keys to a purposeful life
Smiles aplenty minimal strife
No fear of future remorse for past
Security you feel will last

No chatter dancing on brain
Sleeping a quiet refrain
Those you love safe from harm
Those you love keeping you warm

Life and nature congruent
Activities so fluent
Smooth in your stride
Joy emerges from inside

Smile reflects inner glow
Surroundings enthrall you so
Big heart carrying pride
Mirror what's inside

Happenings around at times painful
What you long drives actions gainful
Pulled or twisted by fate
Perspective fills your plate

Grail conquering inner space
Address all concerns you face
Can people around the world
Step out of incessant swirl

Know giving is real
Enjoy that good you feel
Nurture seeds your broadcast
Beam all over make it last

When we do earth will change
Every cell will rearrange
Simple blessing for each day
Hold onto your shining way

What do you do to make each day good?
How do you shift focus from self to others and what do you like about that?

19 CALM

Why only a periodic visit
Inside senses contentment
Better to be the presence often
In a harsh world you soften

Why abandon a simple good deed
There is solace you need
Every step not productive gainful
OK to avoid painful

Practices bring to bear
How to listen and truly hear
Stay calm in the storm
Centered in chatter's norm

Develop practices faithfully adhere
Get off the wheel find calm here
Meditation yoga walk in woods
No need for all the shoulds

You can always find
Rewards of peace of mind
Every day no matter resistance
Benefits of your persistence

What centering practices do you use for balance?
What motivates you to develop them?

20 SPIRITUALITY

Now in this moment and time
Put aside yours I'll put aside mine
Share old ways a sacred warm bath
Invest your being on a lighter path

Way of true heart often a test
Trusting integrity enabling best
Honor spirit lying within
Powerful voices share their whim

Not everyone some won't abide
Destiny beckons the fearful hide
For the faithful earnest true
Spirit guides always renew

Think of many locked in chains
When lonely our energy wanes
Bars not jailers holding them back
Thoughts mindsets prevent a tack

Value wisdom entrusted to you
Deep inside core always knew
Energy reflects essence of you
Follow your path others will to

What did you come to share?
How canyou do that, and what are consequences of not enabling that purpose?

21 LOVING

Powerful force it's the glue
Bonds all together tethers me to you
Powerful verb intention trumps nerve
Fear will disturb stealing your verve

Pulls forward holds back
Progressing on track
Licks wounds salves ills
Enables shuddering chills

Wisdom lies at loving's core
Opening door after door
Teaches folly of pretensions
Surprises in many dimensions

To have let go to get give
Its kindling a reason to live
Honor its presence know it's cure
Revere the elixir keep giving more

Asks all simple profound
Soars heavenly feet on ground
Loving embraces shine your path
Enjoy divine love a mystical bath

Do you feel love in you as energy?
How will you cultivate and harness without an object and use it for good?

22 MEASURED

Life flies by at a harrowing pace
Opposing any state of grace
Driven by profit fueled by power
Little time to rest an hour

Reflect on most creative time
Discover pure thoughts sublime
Emerged from deepest wells
When quiet not answering bells

Another side also true
Trouble emerged out of a rue
Bubbling brew churning quick
You're stuck in a cauldron thick

Chance to honor a truth
Spinning fast you act like youth
Frustrated demanding tense
Scant patience when so dense

Frenzied feeling pressured
Addled mind not measured
Thoughts spin out of control
Paralyzed can't see a shoal

If you reflect when disappointed
Decisions actions not anointed
Navigating serious space
Slow the pace remember grace

What drives the pace you navigate life?
Moving fast as choice or habitually in bubbling soup?

23 TIDES

Bodies are rhythmic like earth
Blossoms harvest summers worth
Heat of summer slows down
Freezing winter don't move around

Ebbs flows within
Mind of their own no whim
Mistake many make
Reasons in life's wake

Objectifying mood we're in
Cause some external whim
Not about this that whatever
Inside like the weather

Embrace or not that's how it is
Resist life says none of your biz
The thing to do if you want peace
Accept rhythms let go release

Only way out is through
Go with flow don't resist what's true
Rhythms your teacher ally friend
Bumps emerge for you to mend

In the end nowhere to go
Home in skin perhaps you know
Welcome friends emerging within
Hug and kiss embrace as kin

Ever think biochemistry causes your internal state and not something external?
How would life change if you honored that?

24 CONNECTIONS

Hold us together keep us alive
Foundation on which we thrive
Reveals essence exposes core
Lights passage that we're here for

Cost of admission only your soul
Whatever it takes keep yourself whole
Longing searching reaching your end
Open to connection anyone is friend

Joyous vibrations warm deep heart
Inspire being helping your art
Populate poetry visions profound
Sourced from love on sacred ground

All beauty serenity peace
Out of synapses quieting your beast
Not about you but what you give
Join others in learning to live

Enjoy connections relish with pride
Puff out your heart savor the ride
Clear what fuels you're not alone
Deeply entwined circle and roam

How does connectivity fuel the quality of your life?
What do you consciously do to increase connectivity?

25 ENERGY

Welling inside power of presence
Palpable force projecting essence
There each moment residing within
Call on it daily it's not a whim

Vibrations reveal the you that's real
Who you are stronger than steel
Never abandons you might leave it
Happens when deceived by your wit

Hiding not feeling strong
Losing direction where you belong
Head to a forest alone is best
Lie down be quiet give self a rest

Breathe in trees inhale mountains
Let them inside filling your fountains
Blue sky fills your aching heart
Whistling wind a new song and start

Nature's forces restore who you are
Revealing truth no searching too far
This energy a source of power
Like a redwood tall every hour

Are you aware of nature's powerful renewal?
What are ways you can tap into it?

26 MEDITATION

Intention presence each moment
Focusing love the now of atonement
Sacred quiet listen to breathing
Sensual air over nostrils streaming

Exploring shores unknowing
Participate in your disowning
Circle back to beginning
Discover source of your winning

Wanting joy in expression
Live in humble self-possession
No need surrender essence
Gift of you wrapped in presence

Don't seek better answer
Find in your sacred dancer
Not in possessions or activity
Not an object of productivity

Dancing quiets in translucency
Find the castle of your fluency
Temper yourself with foundation
Quiet joy true elation

Do you seek, discover and cultivate personal presence?
Can you uncover the pure you?

27 POETRY

Job of a poet let the poems write
Get out of the way despite fright
Poems a gift from far away
For the poet writing is play

Never work no task for brain
Transcribe thoughts sun or rain
Mystery of origin readily clear
Arrives from places far and near

Poems write themself
Ask and they reflect
Seek express essence pure
Hearts' desire wanting more

Economical words where you live
Piercing and you want to give
No longwinded flowery prose
Listen heed oracle knows

Done as writer reader
Taste seems so much sweeter
Life lived close to core
Gifts experiences many more

Experience of poetry for you?
When sharing how do others respond and make you feel?

28 MIND

Torture a mind can unleash
Not feeding hunger or release
Stuck ness holds like a vise
Monkey mind thinks 2X twice

Life better than chattering hell
More letting go makes you well
Hearing the internal storm
Way beyond normal norm

No chatter in north-pointing nod
Joy in the presence of god
No place so deeply home
Presence without scream or moan

Resting firmly feet on ground
Solid nothing to be found
Rich dwelling in your being
Enabling a force they're seeing

From that presence all unfolds
Younger older on your roads
Suddenly quiet chatter abated
Peace alights angels mated

*Do you identify with these words and the impact of presence beyond
thinking mind?*
Do you allow that to inform your search for Peace?

29 KINSHIP

Keeps us alive holds us together
Intact no matter weather
Brings sunshine sends away pain
No matter barometer or forecast rain

Holding a hand kissing a lip
Catches you with a startle or blip
Darkest nighttime blackest hour
Presence a sparkling meteor shower

Amazing simple hearts connected
Love connections feel respected
Connected meanings are a source
Wide smile on your face of course

Sense of traction feeling held
Holding together perfect meld
Infinite variety yours for taking
Crosses boundary's its' generating

Bridges ethnicity religion race
Underlying lattice our grace
When feeling down alone
Loving kinship draws you home

How do connections sustain and provide solace in challenging times?
How do you reciprocate and what's the reward?

30 CENTERED

Many choices little time
This moment reach for divine
Life splayed before you
Contemplate what next to do

No glory waiting here today
Not tomorrow grab the day
Many answers you have keys
Life beckons get up off your knees

Be thoughtful make a plan
Only do what you can
When thinking clouds your brain
Take a slicker don't fret rain

Stay aware god lives in you
No worries for what you want to do
Inspiration in your master voice
Hold perspective always choice

Rarely about yesterday's child
Honor daydreams sometimes wild
Let go of visions once entertained
Be a presence maintained sustained

What keeps you centered and grounded?
What affirmation invokes powerful presence?

July

1 CROSSROADS

At this junction
Choices without compunction
What to choose what's the plan
Direction for woman and man

Lifetimes experiences illusions
Navigated untold confusions
Sitting in 21st millennium
Direction or swinging pendulum

A life lived humdrum
Never appealed an end run
Never faced choices presented
Vision never fermented

Option to be bold
Stay the course break the mold
Tacks to choose every day
Many paths OK to pray

What's my vision and legacy
A will or gold security
Bottom line I must say
Choices that reflect my way

On the verge of morning
What to carve this dawning
Money a cause my art
Always honor sacred heart

Standing at a crossroads what factors do you look at and how do you decide?
Does your process serve you and what do you need to change?

2 CONSEQUENCES

Many choices served by life
Go left up down right
No right answer always true
Let go to what calls you

Ponder indecision
Mulling each revision
Onward upward quest gold ring
Home hearth what's your thing

Words make sense no doubt
They won't figure it out
No equation sorts the wedges
Weighs consequence knows edges

Decide let go feel the pain
No matter newness potential gain
Make choices decide move
Leave behind what you lose

Going forward mind the rain
Always yours no matter fame
Sentient beings discovering worth
Part of living learning earth

Transitions part of the game
Loneliness tears scars shame
Simple answers very clear
Tough ones ponder year on year

Allow all voices listen to heart
Paint your canvas live your art
In the end go to grave
With all you received all you gave

When you leave something how do you feel?
How do you process loss, what does it teach and how does it inform
future passages?

3 GRATITUDE

Thankful I don't ask for more
People presence opening doors
Exciting elations relationship brings
Provides learning so many things

Privilege pleasure engaging deep
Connections make a faint heart leap
Communion of gathering beings
Enables flight they are wings

Grateful for all who hear
Listening to a voice sincere
We can give more than we know
In openness we serve and grow

Grateful boundaries disappear
As you listen and truly hear
What passes between more than gold
Alchemy of presence slows getting old

Thanks to source for dear friends
Without connections at loose ends
Joy pervades when souls touch
For this treasure thank you so much

*Can you be more deliberate generating the joy, healing and discovery
connections bring?*
Can you increase the presence of sacred relating?

4 ESSENCE

At the center heart
Caring with tears and art
No simple answers on earth
Each day delivery birth

Life situations teach
Chart direction reach
Experiences point the way
Grope answers in your play

Gusto intensity living brings
Trying this that drink of things
Glory inside never fades
Even battered by the shades

Long run return to godhead
Pure spirit lives essence fed
Pretend what you have is real
Dream states reflect what you feel

Chances taken journey you follow
Perfect though can be hollow
Purpose of living not material gain
Power of presence in pleasure pain

Are you pushing edges and testing your expansion or playing safely?
Can you courageously go deeper and wider?

5 BURNING

Finally quiet no chatter inside
Stillness at last in which to reside
Dancing brain alights on a perch
Seeing landscapes abound on earth

Journey's thrilling ups downs
Hearty laughter long sad frowns
Frantic activity meant to distract
While anguish resides inside intact

One day wake quiet within
Hit bedrock or just a whim
Knowledge comes after a time
Playing over in circular mind

It does matter it is up to you
Quiet seed inside your brew
Give that quiet nurture galore
Feed with care to give you more

Payoff a healthy glow within
In each cell where fire begins
The spiral flame glows even keel
Sustaining all in you that is real

When you get quiet can you sense bedrock under the chatter?
How do you access that more often?

6 REVELATIONS

What path are you walking
Follow it to find your talking
Many years many storms
Where is a life with norms

One day wake from a dream
Peace inside know what I mean
Deep calm inner tranquility
Finally equanimity

Dreams dreamed prayers prayed
Answered how your game is played
Move forward let it come through
Be the channel so much to do

No longer stress strife
Clear that was no life
Gone that greatest gift
Struggle gone a major lift

Not a whim of thoughts sensations
Now guided by revelations
Devoting life to sacred call
Gifts come through give to all

Has your path been revealed and how did you know it was for you?
If not how might you receive such revelation?

7 KNOWING

Physical comfort illusory serene
A vision from a perfect dream
Lifts gently sets you down
Through portals to a higher ground

Finances or creativity
Things familial or nobility
In your children nature's bliss
Full-bodied cab your lover's kiss

Awards recognitions fame
Headline news name in the game
Doing that quiets down
Try being when no one's around

What questions to ask
In inquiry what's the task
Clear what you need to grow
Filling your heart to overflow

Tumblers unlock you find
Fulfillment in your mind
Living from self-generation
That knowing your elation

What generates clarity about how things fit, their priority and value?
How do you cultivate that state?

8 PERSISTENCE

Accomplishment doing great
Never stop at a locked gate
Push through climb steep steps
Have resolve blame no one else

Understand mission vision
Outcomes without indecision
Develop mindset transcend big hills
No stopping for cold and chills

Dig deeper call on reserves
Find edges of ignited nerves
At outset talk and chatter
Learn how that noise matters

Thwarted in your quests
Time to engage your best
No a sign more demanded
Never leave empty-handed

On this rock in space
Persistence reveals your grace
Anything worth thoughts supreme
Give it all make real a dream

Have you thought about the grit of resilience?
Knocked down, what gets you back up?

9 BUZZING

Buzzing around the globe
Buzzing's getting old
Flying on adrenals to a new perch
Suddenly aware incessant search

Stop the buzzing feet on ground
No more game of lost and found
Gambits of our living games
Who what goes who what remains

Next rarely certain scant clarity here
Speculate what happens next year
Take a moment slow chattering mind
Shut down the quest so you find

Interesting to get off the spin
Few know you're gone or when
Inclined again mount your steed
In not knowing you've been freed

Feeling weary an exhausted soul
Get off the cyclone time to be whole
Gather fractured feelings spirits from afar
Consolidate essence in your jeweled jar

Have you been buzzing and need renewal time?
How does retreat enable contribution to others and self, and what's in the way?

10 COURAGE

Be courageous to live more
In places you've not been before
With real power not fake
Enabling others quiets your wake

Courage motivates exploration
Risk generates failure elation
Launch from uncomfortable stands
Essential for crossing new sands

What you seek in transitions
Motivates actions and decisions
Life on the other side
Richer filling you with pride

Seeing places you want to go
Feel fear gripping you so
To get where you want to be
Find deeper center power is free

Transition about your mind
Shift perspective or stay behind
Break through what holds you back
Gather courage from a muscular tack

*What ways has fear held you back and how has courage contributed to
your life?*
What needs courage in your life today?

11 CREATIVES

Some simple life routine every day
Wake up goodnight no change or play
Others revel in excitement of new
Adding spices to their private stew

Brew drink the soup you stir
Constant change sometimes a blur
Artists thrive on invention
Living in movement without pretension

Creatives rarely stand still
Experiment newness discovery thrill
Eating fish each Thursday night
Makes them crazy they take flight

Freedoms' essence make life anew
Shape shift rearrange transformation too
Bleeding edge pioneers
Their reframes we stand with cheers

Remake a future for all
Elegantly lead standing tall
Notice these magical beings
Acknowledge applaud and say nice things

Do you cling to yesterday's routine, love the thrill
of being on roller skates or something in between?
Is it an automatic preference or consciously chosen?

12 RAIN

Cleansing earth renewing air
Sun's intensity much to bear
Fosters reflection looking within
Nurtures essence when feeling thin

Cooling bubbling quiets inside
Slowing the body from a fast ride
Liquid life elixir sweet wet heals
Without rain earth cracks and peels

Parched dehydrated dry to bone
Quenching nectar quiets your moan
Collecting cisterns reservoirs fill up
Preserving hoarding to fill your cup

Manna from heaven sent by gods
Fattening sweet peas in little pods
Can't live without more than a few days
It disappears we dance shamans pray

Next time upset when wet falls
Soaks a hairdo puts things on pause
Recall sweet scents and vibrant colors
Sun comes out drying druthers

What can rain teach us?
What long-term benefit will remain?

13 REVERENCE

In your reflective side
Feelings won't let you hide
Lingering events from the past
Impact present moving fast

Startled awake new thinking bold
Tempered by mundane joy on hold
Serenity you came to know
Vanished now where to go

Let the lessons reverence brings
Sink deeply thoughts have wings
Insides awaken a new voice
Honor spirit you have no choice

Let emotions purify cleanse
Wisdom emerges to serve those ends
Take heart in a sense of profound
Let knowledge keep you on the ground

Honor the presence of sacred space
Allow ancient wisdom feel the grace
Enable the being that manifests you
Embrace softness let yours through

Do you listen, hear, act on lessons residing in you?
What's in the way and what do you need to access resident wisdom?

14 TECHNOLOGY

Magical gift of tools invented
Menial tasks boredom prevented
Convenience in so many ways
Medical technology airplane delays

Help what's not easy to do
Information connections too
Lack of facts abated
Rural urban divide eradicated

Total reliance caution in order
Y2K an example disorder
Stay mindful of all AI
Keep your head out of the sky

Network breakdowns sabotage
Things go awry feel the barrage
Other fears darker insidious
Diluting human connection serious

A life source energy exchange
Electricity of flesh cells interchanged
All alone plugged to a machine
Eros connection a historic dream

How do you use technology and how does it serve you?
Do you balance life online with face to face connections?

15 FLOW

Roll with punches go with flow
Admonitions truth we know
Find balance as worlds rearrange
Watch expectations feeling strange

Conscious projections mind's eye prelude
In psychic dimensions your world renews
Sacred predictions dimensions profound
Unconscious impacts what is around

The world you know shifting shape
Be present observe with mouth agape
Incremental sneaks up on you
At times be radical profound taboo

Cannot always predict for sure
As you open door after door
At times deny what's up for you
Delaying the future spoiling the new

Within a changing life
Holding on causes strife
Reduce resistance maximize flow
Coast on currents grow and glow

Do you know when you are in a state of flow?
How can you consciously chose to get in and out of the way?

16 DEMONS

Big punch in my solar plexus
Betrayals are the nexus
Long to be anywhere else
Futile to escape from self

Why it comes where to hide
Is there any god inside
Long for stress free quiet peace
Seek a transformational release

Feeling the disease within
Masked well but veneer is thin
Essential now to make peace
Or sadly this life will cease

How to move through the pain
Battle demons pelting rain
Endure without coming undone
Search for strength a little fun

Choices not sure what to do
Face the fear fake it through
I know it's a transient state
I will endure to the next gate

What internal demons have you battled?
What strategies have you used and what was your self-talk?
Can you help others?

17 LIVING

Essence of a life that's human
For every man and woman
Living a privileged existence
Passing uniquely among us

Cherish honor the reverential
Lives we lead great potential
Our biological machines a gift
Amazing vehicle provides lift

Ability to think emote choose
Reflect on a state of win or lose
Attract repulse taste touch smell feel
Experience senses intuit heal

See the missing in cultural mores
Commit to follow a worthy cause
Joy of savoring many flavors
Honor choices minimize waivers

Remorse learning changing doing
Sacrifice for others' pursuing
Sharing pain of injured others
Tending troubled sisters brothers

Passing time cannot be denied
Careful of arrogance pride
Authenticity draws to our fold
Peaceful quiet growing old

What do you want to experience in human form to have a fuller life?
What's lost if you miss the opportunity?

18 INFERIORITY

Judging people a nasty deed
Clearly a destructive seed
Someone worse or better than you
Righteous glorify what they do

Folks have tools inner skills
Personal success developed wills
Raise self push down someone
Based on where they come from

Not about the oppressed
Oppressor's need to be best
Inferior misguided self
Needs bettering or else

Can't succeed by themselves
They oppress for happiness
Masking a missing piece
Hiding pain they can't release

When feeling airs of another
Show compassion be a brother
Rather than raise their life
Deflect demonize be right

Undertake honor pure
See emptiness be a cure
Extend forgive empathy a guide
So sad they live on false pride

See missing pieces in people who raise themselves by making others less?
How can you be more compassionate?

19 HOMECOMING

Caught in the fast spinning wild
Internal external guiding the ride
Agitation anxiety angst loneliness
Fear at times a thrownness

Though I have resources
Can't transcend powerful forces
Suddenly funk over me
One minute coasting next can't see

Just when thinking I escaped
Here taste this on your plate
What causes dizzy spinning
Approaching my ninth inning

Familial patterns thick as glue
Visiting home not yet thru
Memories clouded seductive
Can't let go what I'm up against

Push pull the same breathe
Terrain has little happiness
I want sweetness time after time
Will there ever be sublime

Is visiting family different from what you want?
Can you let expectations go and be with what is?

20 SLOWER

For a child an hour forever
Week an eternity a year life's endeavor
Growing older opposite true
What took patience in no time through

Getting near a date with fate
Time quickens near a pearly gate
Like gravity falling toward the ground
Closer to impact faster hurtling down

Initial knee jerk of most
Push faster never miss a toast
Helter-skelter place to place
Never slow embracing grace

Here to there to outrun
Quantity dilutes deeper fun
Perhaps turn step aside
Off the treadmill slower ride

Savor taste each bite
Enjoy flavors travel light
Wake up on the other side
Engagement a more graceful ride

Are you tasting life or moving too fast?
What do you want to savor and how can you do that?

21 DISTRIBUTION

Rage inside hardly stops
God laughs our species flops
Planet a gift of sacred trust
Let's harness intention and thrust

Leaves on trees shrivel die
All this prosperity yet we cry
Potential's promises denied
Where is genius and pride

Bombing easy explode the moon
Much at peril heading to ruin
Enough boy toys time to grow wise
Allow compassion see rage in eyes

Missiles cause much greater harms
Look for solutions no dropping bombs
Invite wise women we know
Steward the planet run the show

With intuition feminine wiles
Forget politics turn rage to smiles
Realize what doesn't serve
Discover while keeping verve

War's not the answer only brings more
Enemies remember revenge finds a door
Dooming children to a grave with fear
Why not a heart song salvation's so near

Enough for all more than enough
Explore how to care not being tough
All people want to bloom in life
Food shelter learning peace little strife

All deserve safety opportunity to grow
Abundance here in a paradise we know
Our resources more than enough
Distribution the challenge deliver right stuff

Resource or distribution challenge?
If you were in charge what priorities would you use for planetary resources?

22 SECURITY

Longing for a place to rest
Letting down serves us best
Basic needs met each day
Trust the future why not play

Looking for a place of home
Bedrock from which to roam
All cradled in what seems
Tranquility of our dreams

Where to find build hold it
Nurture every component
Best part painted scenes can heal
Ground makes you more real

Folly we share seek to find
Something not of our mind
After searching years all over
Find it inside to uncover

Security lies in trusting essence
Closely listen you're the reference
When feeling lonely afraid small
Honor your voice it provides all

What is security and home for you?
If you had it would your life be different and can you honor what's inside?

23 PILGRIMS PATH

Alone we're born alone we die
Within aloneness sometimes cry
Much of life is illusion
Fighting our inner confusion

Not so frequent oneness visits
Then we know the wholeness in us
Periodically wake from the dream
Clear about your sweet machine

Lessons on pilgrim's path
Stay mindful when feeling wrath
Only in body we get to feel
Lower emotions animal sphere

Life can be tough on the human plane
Contrast unity from the spirit we came
Another dimension place called home
Never alone part of the whole

Unity's memory of life on earth
No matter nobility or common birth
Search for a path back to god
Not so serious please wink and nod

Can you see living in body a context to feel, explore and learn about self and emotions?
Are scorecards and achievement so important?

24 MINDFULNESS

Best presence to carry along
Connect to your sweet song
Embody aliveness whatever you do
Everyday old suddenly new

Engage deeply with self and others
Be a source healing druthers
Longing that drives filled in a minute
Clinging subsumed when you're in it

Mindful presence honors all things
Acknowledges humanity tempers feelings
Shifts energy requiring attention
Transports to another dimension

Why choose anything different
A world with what you want in it
Present to what surrounds
Receive create what abounds

No sitting sorry for self
Go out give to someone else
Giving to others what you need
Manifests what you want to receive

Are you aware of concern you have for others,
your generosity of spirit and the pleasure of giving?
Does the law of reciprocity give what you want to receive?

25 POWER

Rocket power fuels propulsion
Here to there swift eruption
Motivates pulls pushes
Moves you when stuck in bushes

Force inside your strength and will
Vision drives while standing still
Mission here essence actions tasks
Cause to live for continually asks

Heart fuels wakening thoughts
Brings more treasure than ever sought
Stronger than steel no bend or break
Can't burn or scratch won't even flake

Tap into your sacred source
Guiding life rarely remorse
Nuclear reaction inside you
Erupting exploding empowering too

The promise to you for sure
Emergence unlocks a sacred door
Coiled tightly rising taking flight
Awake all day and night

Right action what is it for you
Inner wisdom knows what to do
Voices share wisdom of the heart
Let power within turn life to art

What lights your fire and keeps you motivated?
How do you feel in that space and what emerges?

26 POROUS

Less to be more
Less dense what life's for
Be nothing transparent clean
Quiet catalyst unseen

Impact without being influential
Impact and consequential
Move mountains singing a sweet tune
Blow bubbles on warm days in June

In solace and quiet reverie
Tears stop yearning finally free
Engagement connection collaboration
Something big in your elation

Joy waiting wide as sky
Still empty quiet oh my
No sparkle or bombast profound
Slowly traversing sacred ground

Go forward looking for ease
Dance lightly say thank you please
Float engage with a light hand
Resistance dissolves to grains of sand

Where are you strident and serious, where a sense of "lightness of being?"
Which is more hospitable and productive?

27 INTEGRITY

Congruent within and without
Integrated toes to mouth
Powerful gait and voice
It is never a choice

Not image or strategic vision
How you live clarity precision
End of day finish labor
Lie down rest warmth savor

Who you are what you do and say
Your word a bond of honor each day
Called upon feed the poor
Nurture what walks in your door

Living from inside out
Heart your guide no twist or shout
Your truth and belief
Vow and action brings relief

No mercenary ambition
Dedicated to your mission
Nearing end look back reflect
Lived your dream no repent

Does your life aspire to the poetic aspirations?
Can you live more from the inside out of your integrity?

28 PLACE

Home ground rest stillness
Comfortable no willfulness
All quiet close to heart
Begin again a new start

Life meets us under feet
Feeling heart rhythmic beat
Belongings found here
Stuff provides cheer

Go home for rebirth
Arrive for joy and mirth
Does not matter time of year
Place of grounding never fear

Dear heart do you have a home
A longing space when you roam
A spot drawing magnet's pull
Showing up you are full

Life has purpose in this space
Creative visions provide grace
Profound meaning for your heart
Balance resides no fits or starts

Where is home for you and what happens there?
Would visiting serve you?

29 PERSPECTIVE

Perspective an important tool
Keeps you from being a fool
When thinking things are low
Reality perhaps not so

Who better who worse
Without comparison a curse
Despair for your plight
Without perspective's light

Feeling sad it's not so bad
Others wish what you had
Walk on any urban street
Realize it's not so bleak

Notice homeless all around
Tattered vendors in the crowd
Aged disabled disfigured and such
Suddenly blessed with so much

Task at hand for you to see
Privilege deserves some glee
Do not mope become unglued
Look at life be amused

How does comparing your life to homeless, war, disease shift your assessment?
Does perspective provide a new view?

30 JAZZ

This moment in time
Right now all is fine
Not forward backward aft or stern
Deep in body where we learn

No chatter vibrating the brain
Silence quiet each cell the same
Can you focus like this all the time
Moment to moment in perfect rhyme

Presence of now power that's you
Concentrated seeing you through
No matter what's served on life's plate
Digesting time makes it taste great

Security purpose and mission
Focused ready for any transition
Life's changes come and go
Attitude a vehicle that matters so

Things unfold go fast and slow
Faith your beacon follow its glow
Return to center careful of drift
Allow your jazz play a great riff

What songs do you need to write so you can play them?
What story do you want to share in what tone and mood?

31 LONGING

Pain in the soul
Where you're not whole
Slice missing in your heart
Motivates action stimulates art

In the center of your source
Life's connected no remorse
Healing driver reigns supreme
Congealing you a human being

Longing says incomplete
Emptiness moves your feet
Right direction head true north
Honor purpose holy trough

Beauty is your sacred womb
Choosing freedom or a tomb
In your time on this rock
Cogitate and take stock

Here you search and cajole
Honor ponder divine soul
Think about the deep divorce
Be fortunate reconnect to source

Connected to an inner or external source?
Does that source ground, heal and keep you connected?

August

1 SIMPLICITY

Down at essence center core
Remember what you came for
Beneath chatter running about
Quiet simplicity wants to shout

Artists work reduce refine
A grand epic to a line
One brush stroke a simple word
Enduring for all who heard

Truth is simple without noise
Emerges out of your poise
Natural shapes you can see
Open heart frees you to be

Complexity much to do
Then get older wiser too
Everyday pleasure grist of life
Satisfying little strife

Eating laughing sunset's delight
Communing makes your life bright
Encouragement wisp of touch
Smile teardrop hug says much

Effortless blissful states
Wisdom an abundant plate
Boundless pleasures mostly free
Slow don't try just love and be

Are you taking enough time to enjoy simple pleasures?
How can you engage in a daily simple pleasure and what is today's?

2 SORTING

What stays what goes
What's joy what forebodes
Where do you find footing
Pray for when no one's looking

What blocks movement has you soar
Makes you bolt for the door
Who's handsome who brings a frown
Who's optimistic who turns you down

When lonely fills you up
Brings big smiles when in the cups
Who stimulates engages your mind
Who taps creativity never a grind

These questions essential to ask
Looking for your unique path
Others say do not judge
Sorting's elitist fosters a grudge

We do express ourselves
Choosing what's on our shelves
Never stop picking why even try
Select celebrate what you buy

Your choice never better worse
Only different never a curse
Respect what's on their plate
You won't be held up at the gate

What criteria do you use choosing work, people, possessions,
behavior, character, politicians, movies and reading?

3 TOLLS

Think you have a free ride
Think you could easily slide
Think you could escape your end
Think life always your friend

Quiet delusions put us to sleep
Privileged hiding time to weep
Longing that we all share
Without sacred little here

All pay taxes one or another
Life has tolls pay go under
Passage to the other side
Generates graceful pride

Price we pay as we go
Costs what we don't know
A tax in lieu of learning
We pay to cool our burning

When you begin to really live
Treasure in what you give
Honor friends in your hive
Their nectar keeps you alive

Do you grumble about life's tolls?
When you factor what you receive how does that quiet the chatter?

4 SOLACE

Hurtling in time and space
Search and scan for grace
Look for solace and peace
Find a place for release

Bounce around pillar post
What knowing startles most
Realize all the bouncing
To escape the trouncing

Discover what you search for
Is inside no need for more
Connect to heart in chest
Provides solace serves you best

Mind within thoughts you think
Dramas keep you from your pink
Travel seek as you go
Never better than inside so

Your world mind makes up
Self-talk empowering or rough
Choose to reprogram the brain
Power in you sunshine or rain

What words do you use in shaping your reality?
How can words change relationships, work and well-being?

5 GROUNDING

Life journey seeking center
Thinking it resides in a mentor
Initially parents fill the need
Then religion provides a creed

Political cause an honored dream
Something simple or extreme
Teachers and career goals
Family friends spouses roles

It shifts place to place
Often outside our grace
Notice all these things
External to human beings

As you move about
Learn through all your doubt
Discover your sacred source
Deep inside no divorce

Don't be afraid follow heart
That spark is your art
Why seek external validation
Why not your own inspiration

Is your ground external or internal?
Do you make deliberate choices about your center and do they impact your life?

6 GROWING

Slate is clean ready for new
Delight in a you that's true
Illusion that we're separate
We're connected please accept it

Honor voices of heart mind
Listen to incessant chattering grind
A wellspring tap purest source
Time of action not remorse

Ladle joy scatter magic dust
Repair fissures keep vows trust
Step forward in what you know
Heighten trajectory so you grow

Speak no shyness or hesitation
No passivity in your elevation
Enable presence to come through
Let your choices reveal you

Mindful of clouding true seeing
Quiet ego destroying being
Summon wise sources heed your call
A sacred journey give your all

Do you hold back what you came to give others?
Can you see how care of others cares for self?

7 SAD

When tragedy strikes a lover
Take pain away quiet the thunder
Prefer not to feel hurt sadness sorrow
Beseech the gods change tomorrow

Joy longed for sadly fleeting
Pray for tranquility meeting
Want it to go away without scars
Laugh play romp among the stars

Help them see and know
Life lessons place to grow
No faint of heart or shrinking being
Get to learn eyes opened seeing

Go within for golden threads
Living's not for selfish ends
Honor paths others walk
Cherish them not their talk

Give way more than take
Pay respect stay awake
Rant and rave let all be said
Be with them help the end

Are lessons from your life experience or can you take from lives of others?
Who needs your compassion and empathy now?

8 RICHES

What are riches what is gold
What gives solace growing old
Generates a toothy smile
Comforts only for a while

What is your sacred desire
To what do you aspire
What does your heart treasure
Gives you divine pleasure

What engages all your passion
You give without ration
What do you do for damaged things
That counts among your blessings

Clearly knowing the above
Provides delight and love
Not your bank account
No difference the amount

Money not an end it's means
To accomplish other things
A tool to exchange
Giving you broader range

Funds fuel projects and your vision
Helps you move with more precision
Facilitates your sweet plan
Giving to the family of man

Spending enough time in pleasurable activities?
Do you have gratitude for gifts you provide for others?

9 LISTEN!

Crossroads no opportunity danger
Current time never stranger
Rarely in history
Did humanity face such misery

Where to turn for answers
Amid all around disasters
Search for sages to show the way
Long for guides so daily pray

Standing firm spun around
Moving fast where is ground
When I knew up from down
Without some perpetual frown

Have we all forgotten
What to do what's verboten
Need people we know well
Those we trust to help and tell

Answers inside pay attention
Look within for comprehension
From the dark silence within
Inner wisdom with a sacred grin

Be slow answer what calls
No time for any jerks or stalls
Sooth others from any fall
Take the time answer the call

Do you listen to voices deep inside and take messages seriously?
Why not trust that wise consciousness?

10 IMPROVISATION

Improvisation is being alive
In the moment aspiring to thrive
Living in the heart of life
Beyond fear cutting through strife

No planning or controlling moves
No scripting or suffering fools
Trusting answers do come
Beyond choices having fun

Thoughts sensations effect you
Others' impact what you do
Doing your best fostering wokeness
Create from your personal god sense

Enable a following heart
Let freedom reveal your art
No constrictions stay in flow
Intuition propels your go

Reflect on what you did
Validate aliveness awareness of skid
Let go self-concepts' jailing chains
Allow footsteps to unfold rearrange

Are you open to influence or resist change based on the current reality?
Can you develop the confidence of spontaneity?

11 QUIET

Be still quiet listen to god
Speaking inside your private pod
Providing wisdom and spark
Shining a light when dark

Your path not for the meek
Strength courage continually seek
Strip everything to bone
Who's there when you're alone

Behind your chatter and hum
Beneath knowing where you are from
Deep in caverns of each cell
Far down there you dwell

Visit often this blissful place
As living moves at its frantic pace
Check in know it feels right
Connect to essence day or night

In the recess god bubbles up
Let the nectar fill your cup
Not a grand plan from afar
In quiet splendor you really are

What's required to get still and hear voices deep inside?
What keeps you from that time and space?
Go now!

12 RESILIENCE

Demons of consciousness defy intention
Renders you spineless in a dimension
Cancels self-confident energy of being
Blindfolds vision relegates seeing

Surly monster seems without end
Enveloping demanding you bend
Progress halted actions stop
Life is molasses you want to drop

Will it end this bottomless pit
Will you surface intact with wit
In this chasm been here before
Daunting passage not what you came for

Helping endure seeing the end
Resilience elevates it is a friend
Ordeal ends finally turn
Lessons prevail so much to learn

Life not for the meager or weak
Nor the faint-hearted acting like sheep
Listen to voices follow your heart
Let life come unfolding as art

Cultivate wisdom be kind to friends
Hear with compassion serve make amends
Be patient humble no worry about trends
Take joy in hours connected to friends

How do you get beyond the overwhelm of challenging moods?
Can you anticipate situations knowing you will persevere and thrive drawing
on resilience?

13 EXPANSION

Time to be bigger grow be wise
Time to see clearly head heart eyes
Let go of yesterday's fears
Holding you back many years

Step into your sacred now
Present moments let you know how
Reject tentative hesitant no
You have power make it all so

It's not magic or sense of pride
You came with purpose no longer hide
Start singing the song that is you
Deliver wisdom until you are through

Find the chorus waiting for you
They cheer and support when you are blue
No need to linger it's already so
For eons you've been kneading the dough

Be clear of purpose with a strong will
Resolve uncertainty manifest cure what's ill
Allow beauty and wisdom you are
To permeate others and carry far

Fill up what's missing abundance here now
The gift of giving serves others and how
Transcend challenges enlarge and surround
Let love encompass permeate and abound

Where do you need to expand?
What fears haveprevented you from evaluating risks and taking action given
what's at stake?

14 BIFURCATION

What a wish and longing
Two places each belonging
Feeling pulled sometimes twisted
Want to be here go there missed it

Many times frustrated
When I ought to be elated
How do I succeed
One part wants the other pleads

What to do what solution
From conundrum to resolution
Simple answer easy clear
Both places with good cheer

Hindu masters had an answer
Resourceful intention avoid disaster
Clarity of spirit force of will
Went both places had their fill

Physical body sent one place
Spirit elsewhere went with grace
Intention for what happened there
Physical body calmly here

To some folly mere delusion
Hocus pocus just illusion
Others sure with clarity rare
Both places easy just be there

Where did you learn to deal with conflict and is your mindset serving you?
Can you choose to creatively manage conflict?

15 COMPASSION

Be human nurture who's here
Care share express good cheer
Quietly know longing of other
Mother father sister brother

No need to cultivate
Born within part of your gait
Lives in marrow and gene
Inhabits soul powerful meme

When others do untoward action
Don't give their behavior traction
Push back at their choice
Get bigger prevent remorse

Discern who's over there
Reflect on story listen hear
Where do they come from
Motivation and intention

Gather perspective understand
Give of yourself without demand
Compassion is who you are
Give freely you will travel far

Do you put yourself in others' shoes before making judgments?
How does judging vs. learning impact relationships?

16 GROUNDED

Grounded feet on floor
Never been fully here before
Deep in body belly home
From this center I can roam

Path traveled tacks and stalls
Speeding mountains slamming walls
Midnight sweating hole in chest
Ongoing longing place to rest

Reclaim being that's pure
Rearranged do not want more
Life in body challenges too
Earth a teacher wisdom school

Many resist process of living
Experience can be unforgiving
Engage embrace you that's real
Let go defenses trust and feel

Birthrights gift a life sublime
Follow heart song enjoy time
Greatest knowing inside you
Deep in body friend lover too

Have a sense of being fully seated in your body?
Can you appreciate and pay tribute to the wisdom the body holds?

17 HEAVEN

What's heaven or hell
Wherever thoughts dwell
In the air on the ground
Objective reality rarely found

Perspective generates emotion
You control locomotion
Any circumstance
You decide the dance

See with eyes hear with ears
Self-talk creates loves fears
Can you see the pull
Glass half empty or half full

You choose how you think
Change your life in a blink
Stay present shift self-talk
Words within change your walk

Remember life is a dream
Act write produce direct the screen
Experience heaven or hell
Wisely select stories you tell

Are perspectives you honor yours or others?
Given power to choose how might you shift self-talk, perspective and
world view?

18 PROFIT

Measure worth of endeavor
Keep accounts be clever
Usual metric of profit loss
ROI bank account's boss

How about other indicia
Caring for brother sister
Balance acts that are wise
Need currency for supplies

Comprehensive tallying sheet
New gauge what a treat
Measure value of other people
Helping them climb their steeple

Count smiling faces around
Of good work we are proud
A human capital account
See it bulge growing stout

As finances grow abundant
Why not have some fun with it
Lessons learned as we reflect
Not hard to add self-respect

What metrics build a balance sheet for your life?
What metrics might you add?

19 PRIORITIES

What's first what's last
Important abiding fizzles fast
Gets attention amid the calling
What is rising what is falling

Demands presence object of focus
Holds you tight in its locus
Provides satisfaction and returning
Heart longs with your yearning

Rings a bell in a discerning mind
Fades with distance left behind
You've answered the above
Pointings to things you love

May I suggest being bold
Smarter as you grow old
Periodically inquire ask
Keep around not likely last

Important for you to know
Fill life with what makes you glow
Fill your days with delight
Sleep soundly and rest well at night

Surrounded by people that make you glow or do you have sorting to do?
How would life be different if you were surrounded by energy and inspiration?

20 PEOPLE

Others energy our source
Dear one's spark life of course
When low needing strength
Giving provides what's heaven sent

Connections permeate deep inside
Our source of wisdom and pride
What we have not who we are
Relationships our lucky star

Brothers sisters around
Life gets whole above ground
Reflect what's close to home
Engage give never alone

Measure what you really have
Always be other's salve
Stay mindful realize truth
Giving is getting says super sleuth

Meaning increases as others take
More we give more we wake
Others a path to sacred soul
Dear ones your greater whole

Are you good at enabling others to define yourself?
Who are you without them in your life?

21 INTEGRATION

Trunk of redwood robust ballast
Others prosper drink from your chalice
Firm in presence sure of way
Comfortable steady rock in fray

Solid emergence taking over
After years tilling undercover
Finally transition inside
Within turns no longer hide

Dynamic presence standing strong
No fleeing know you belong
Rooted in wisdom values like rock
Steady pace like tick of clock

Power frightens vibe scares others
Especially those filled with druthers
Others admire things you do
Stay mindful all's not about you

Primary focus giving to others
Make sure they're ok sisters brothers
Traveling a path you scythe
Aware that narrow thought divides

What else might you do to take care of closest people,
those in the next circle out and folks you do not know?

22 LAUGHTER

Best medicine for the heart
Laughter always a new start
Recycle head heart brain
Robust reboot pause refrain

Takes you to sacred core
Place where you were born
Taps back to your foundation
A sacred ground of elation

Immediate smile on your face
A lightening moment of grace
Embodies a knowing grin
Shifts losing to a big win

Laughter is proof god's around
Wakes brain cells so profound
Reminds what lives in your soul
Chuckles cackles a new whole

Your glory clear pure clean
Awake in a rebooted machine
Laughter scrubs the grime
Clears all gunk returns to prime

What generates laughter for you?
How do you stay mindful of that power and ensure that presence in your life?

23 MOVE

Movement food for the soul
Tonic for thirst to be whole
Shifting energy shifting stance
Shifting footsteps a new dance

Choose cheerful or sad
Choose empty or glad
Observe feelings passing through
Full empty chalice of you

Doubt toss turn
Each journey a teacher learn
Access what you need to earn
Wisdom in every yearn

Let steps follow others
Do what attracts without druthers
Honor dances emerging from you
Let motion moderate blue

God is shepherd you're not sheep
Many a guide no reason to weep
One foot another don't need a plan
Start a journey with a sense of I can

What can you change about life when feeling stuck?
What steps can you take and what's the risk?

24 MISSION

Your purpose vision mission
There yet or indecision
A plan at time of birth
For your life on earth

Each has noble work
From that discover worth
Engage with clear intention
Life in another dimension

Discover what's inside
Flight-plan waiting to guide
Sits dormant till awake
When engaged fills your plate

Time digs at your core
Find what you're here for
More clarity with each decision
Trust answers and revision

Distractions of many forms
Look inside for your norms
Keep peeling paring detail
Ears eyes open read email

When keys arrive for bliss
Unlock with a kiss
Live with purpose vision
Honor dreams and your mission

Have you identified your personal mission?
If you think you do not know can you pretend you do?
What is it?

25 LEAPING

Fear's grip holding tight
Muscles freeze icy fright
Futures' void drives unrest
Will you pass the test

No matter times we've been before
Horizon daunts approaching door
What to do where to go
Next step how do you know

Facing a cliff
Retreat after a sniff
From yesterday you came
Seeing now a new frame

Self-talk holds us back
From leaping to our next tack
Faith of footsteps what you need
Trust a trapeze will catch indeed

Turn to future embrace with joy
Welcome the unknown a play toy
Fill voids with masterful mind
Leave whimpering clinging behind

Is fear in the way of next steps?
Does evidence support the fear and is there a real risk?

26 LAWYERS

Only facts need to know
Courtrooms a big ego show
Talk talk talk rarely listen
Heart is shut hair does glisten

Language sometimes arcane
Pomposity air of urbane
Smoke and mirrors to fluster
Arrogant amid bluster

Caught in a nasty pinch
No room to give an inch
Pledge to give all they can
Loyalty a fist with a plan

Choose correctly follow heart
Only one whose life is art
Passion for your cause supreme
Your story is your knights' dream

Think above exaggeration
Caricature to get attention
Ask clients what they think
Love their lawyer nod and wink

* *What's your experience when needing an advocate?*
  What was good, what missing; how and why would you choose differently?

27 MINDFUL

Human capacities set us apart
Characteristics enable art
Not an attribute we can see
Quality of mind sets us free

Most creatures instinct alone
Never reflect discover what's so
Self-aware select a face
Gifts can provide grace

Along with ability to change
Assess behavior rearrange
Choose what we believe
Choices enable us to achieve

Human life not in stone
The mindful can atone
Aware of this and that
Some idea where you are at

Time for new grooves
Want to make some moves
Traverse through dark night
To be true norths' brightest light

Has self-awareness helped make changes in who and what you are?
When you lose who you are how do you get to a preferred self?

28 LESSONS

Here for lessons on earth
Enjoy blessings and mirth
Acquire knowledge learn stuff
Discover balance and what's enough

Pure spirit experience bliss
Little impinges on perfectness
In bodies we understand
Emotions limits frustrations grand

Choose incarnation in body
At times experience is shoddy
Learn when trapped inside
Your vehicle how to drive

Next deal with your brain
Master an intelligence game
Hormones drive you insane
Conundrums creating shame

Flits by quickly spark of living
Choose compassion be forgiving
At last some control
Just in time for growing old

What lessons did you come for?
Is life providing what you need to learn and who to learn with?

29 EXPANDING

Longer I live more I don't know
Simultaneously feeling slow
Memory lapses sometimes a sham
At the same time wonderful I am

Grow expand stretching ends
Opposites giving bends
Without arrogance or conceit
Full of self feels oh so neat

Life unfolds mystery awe
Stay alive learning more
Let go being sure
Not knowing a fine allure

Sweet perfume laser clarity
Same time vaporization polarity
Open receptive search grow
Seek what you cannot know

Wonder ask seek explanation
Understand quiet frustration
Focus on expanding presence
Let days reveal a new essence

What keeps you alive, motivated and excited?
What can you stop and what do more of to stay engaged?

30 MEDITATION

Close to head heart
Peaceful quiet start
Connecting what's real at core
Close to bone you're here for

Noise of silence spacious black
Bottomless empty puts you on track
Not about action getting someplace
More removing uncovering grace

Longing need desire cease
Observer within has far reach
See hear eyes on truth
Discovery your super sleuth

Heaven glory cauldron of hell
At times in your padded cell
Seeing ends depths of worlds
Immersed in your secret swirls

Viewing facets of deep life
Fertile marrow some sacrifice
Want to live in this rich dream
Personal laser knows your scheme

When you arrive says to you
Kudos for getting out of the stew
Honor revelations profound
Beauty of life on ground

Earth an oyster pearls for you
Wisdom reveals what is true
In the moment enjoy grace
Trusting your own inner space

Do you have a meditation or other centering practice?
What does it provide for you?

31 CURIOSITY

Embrace what seems true
Learn from every you
Deeper level of who we are
Learning machines we travel far

Sorting scanning processing
At times obsessing
Curious this drawn to that
Want to know intuition and fact

Youngsters bright inquisitive
Questions never diminutive
Never know who they will be
Einstein Edison Marconi

Greater than just looking up
How does it all hook up
Apply new to old
Having courage being bold

Keep moving to new spheres
Shake stagnation of our years
Exquisite the way we work
Learning the great human perk

What inspires your learning and how do you learn best?
Do you enjoy endorphins learning releases?

September

1 SOURCE

Your center a place of source
From deepest belly a true voice
Longing for wisdom truth
Ideals recalled from youth

Essence a crown jewel inside
Messages your worthy guide
Seek solace so pure
Knowing what you're here for

Traverse life up down
One day failure next a crown
Knowing what you'll be
For causes you cannot see

Wells inside unfold mystery
Things from varied history
Reflecting on your learning rock
Perched where you take stock

Get quiet with your ringing bell
Disquiet subsides sit a spell
Troubled hurting feeling empty
In this place always plenty

Where do you go when off-center, what happens and what questions are useful?
What's received?

2 SOLID

Standing on my feet
No crying whining neat
Recapturing divine essence
Enabling erect presence

No longing others take charge
No dependence that's large
Life-long fear burns away
Truths inside out to play

Journey home back to core
Victory in a great war
Battle struggle test on test
Never over rarely rest

Gestation creates uproar
In a place you've been before
Emergence takes whatever time
Seeking what's already mine

Thrashing mashing gnarling crazed
At last quiet and amazed
Straining stressing all the shout
Let go demons get them out

When they leave what remains
Silent crystal clarity entrained
Guides hold you for sure
Help honor dreams you came for

Journey's rewards are many
Learning worth every penny
Teach others inspire new friends
Light a path for their ends

Have you felt your core and found more layers?
Does that inform your journey?

3 TEACHING

Gift of giving joy and thrill
Stimulation exercising will
Intention from the front of room
Generate a learning vroom

Growth expansion for all present
Student teacher derive benefit
Choice to stand and lead
Even when you think you need

Fearing words won't come
No applause when you're done
Simple though not an easy task
Giving all then you bask

Edutaining theatre sublime
Giving back more each time
Adrenalin no matter how tired
Show time comes you get wired

They learn your heart sings
Questions make your bell ring
Gift of giving joy and smiles
Changing lives for many miles

What is your experience in a teaching role?
How can you be a teacher no matter the job?

4 EFFORT

Satisfaction digging deep
Daily effort before asleep
Healthy empty when spent
Pleased where energy went

Your gifts reason to live
What pulls you to give
Offer freely no holding back
You are on the right track

Reciprocity returns many fold
Reward consolation growing old
Meanwhile feeling good each day
Earned well your daily pay

Belonging sense of pride
You're on the right side
Others see you guide the way
Revealing your holy play

Not money recognition fame
Not ego or your good name
Giving sharing a sweet soul
Helping others to grow whole

What is your gift that provides value?
Will you stay clear about this best work and give freely?

5 ENGAGED

Engaged by something bigger than you
Gripped by a cause pulling you through
Longing supplanted by action profound
Thrusting forward feet on ground

Propelled from inside no fear or complaint
Beyond intention pushed thru a gate
A calling driving steering your ship
Profound navigator attached at the hip

Not tired till out of steam
Moving forward living your dream
Fascinating watching yourself emerge
Smiles enfolding you're on a verge

Destiny's been calling you
In your face no time for blue
Sense of lost griped you in fear
A fading memory as reward is near

Seeker's don't give up rarely give in
Never discount each deserved win
Honor spirit driving inside
Taking you on an E ticket ride

Wisdom intact follow spirits call
Authentic presence will give you all
Cleave to mission let all else recede
Welcome all gifts joyously receive

What engages you deeply, compelling digging in and effort?
What satisfaction is provided and what legacy remains when complete?

6 SABBATH

No matter who or where
As long as there is air
Life does require
Periodic rest from desire

We deserve a day of peace
Let what's relentless cease
Recharge cells relax mind
Give ourselves a taste of kind

Time to sit and cogitate
Reflect on your state of state
Take a big time-out
Ask what's your life about

Time to make your being whole
Refresh body mind and soul
Connect with universal mind
Clear up places that do bind

Renewed back in the chase
Rested ready for your next race
Keep going without a stop
You will hit a wall and drop

Take needed Sabbath time
Helps to make your life sublime
Memories of peaceful rest
Prepare you for your next quest

Do you have renewal practices in your life?
Do they provide enough or do you need more?

7 CENTER

Swirling round twisted brain
Unrelenting torrential rain
Manic baffling you want to shout
Feeling good not all life's about

Beneath commotion deep in mist
Quiet beyond analysis
Eye of needle center of storm
Respite within providing warm

Burning glow can sustain
Salving aches dries pelting rain
Perspective when frayed and worn
Abiding laughter for your storm

Holy sacred in profane
Helps navigate searing pain
Enshrouds protects essential you
Central kingdom where you rule

Seek abiding peace inside
Quiet feeds cells their pride
Here all worthwhile is born
Holy birthing from your storm

When do you experience the quiet still center of being?
What enabled access, what was generated and how can you return often?

8 SIMPLICITY

The essence of your core
Knows what you're here for
Beneath the chatter running about
Quiet simplicity without shout

Work of artists reduce refine
Express an epic in a line
A brush stroke simple fine
Says much for a long time

Truth is simple no diverting noise
Surfaces from abiding poise
Natures form shapes what you see
Clear hearts' eye frees you to be

Pleasures from the grist of life
Satisfaction little strife
Think its' complex so much to do
Then get older wiser too

Eating laughing sunset's delight
Communion companion delivers light
Smile teardrop a hug says much
Encouraging words a wisp of touch

Effortless blissful states
Wisdom fills abundant plates
Earthly pleasures reasonably free
Slow stop trying love just be

Taking time to enjoy simple pleasures?
How might life change if you engaged one simple pleasure every day?

9 DANCERS

In the preciousness of days
Pause mend habitual ways
Inside lie answers
Many selves the dancers

Something missing there is gain
Beauty living in the pain
Empty feeling is expected
Adjustments then resurrected

Sadness leans over a ledge
Beats falling off the edge
Authenticity takes courage tact
Living is a high wire act

Engage fully each moment
Each step an atonement
Rarely more than you can carry
Though at times it seems scary

Keep going make your mark
Heal be good to your heart
Task always of current times
Making reason with your rhymes

*Are you separated from something important- partner, job, profession,
community, family?*
*Have you explored your self-talk about what happened and what to learn and
digest so you can move on?*

10 PURPOSE

Ancient wisdom of long ago
Footsteps tell us where to go
Laughter wholeness as a guide
Hard to falter god inside

Longing quiet function clear
Purpose revs slip into gear
Journey here filled your life
Awareness travel added spice

Chatter silent systems tight
No bolts rattling at night
Clear as black crystal ice
Context for your next flight

Excited with creative birth
Always hold onto mirth
Sliding to delivery room
Expanse lit by the moon

Don't know each exact move
A trapeze appears all is smooth
Tempered excitement feet on ground
Journeys excite and often astound

Have you trusted a calling you did not fully know but were compelled?
Do you look for guidance from within at a crossroads?

11 PEACE

Peace making a noble art
Inside is the place to start
Motivated to play your part
First look to your heart

Actions reflect an inner smile
Engagement transcend ego's wile
Find in your inner reserves
A driver when you lose nerves

Your humanity pushes this end
Not knowing the next bend
Compassionate wings of dove
Sweet nectar of pure love

Quietly touching inner source
Stop chatter let go of remorse
Vision of peace that abides
Clear about your insides

Faith emerges quieting fear
Trust that you will get there
Narrow steps more steep and true
Mindful counsel it's not about you

Selfless presence guides the way
Vehicle with a sense of play
Silent center chaos all around
Birthing peace on common ground

Have you embraced that your external mirrors the internal?
What is unsettled in your world craving more peace?

12 REBIRTH

Fortunate time on earth
One life many lifetimes worth
One birth incomplete
Many chapters all with feet

Skin I chose confines me
Resist growth never free
Each molt starts within
Shed to go where never been

Change thinking and behavior
Transform inside add new labor
In short time life renewed
Confines gone tether removed

Anyone can renew
A practice not for the few
Step beyond leave old coat behind
Walk naked shed the chattering mind

Many choices on your screen
See scenes of a new dream
Choose context visions emerge
Phoenix rises when submerged

Ready for another life?
What's your vision?

13 TRUTH

Can you face
A life of disgrace
Lost connection to things real
No longer know what to feel

Crowing like I know
Inside feeling low
A charade not forever
Need ballast anchor tether

Here crying inside
Deny sadness with false pride
Heavy heart
Time for new start

Circle of life a wheel
Opportunity to sense feel
Part of journey rise from muck
Extracted from being stuck

One thing certain in life
You'll be tested by the strife
No question sadness difficulty
Can you answer with resiliency

When down use your head
Chose life not the bed
Sad when not feeling great
Reward for patience at the gate

When fearful and desperate what's your self-talk?
Can you embrace your state as a learning for next time?

14 NOW

This moment here now
Stay present it will teach you how
Listen carefully be with what's so
Resist the ease of no

Honor the experience of now
Let life work out somehow
It's not in the future or past
Right now's are all that last

Limit self-talk of yesterday's rain
Clouds pass quickly stay present remain
Secret of freedom and richer life
Present mindfulness eliminates strife

Dancing is only one foot then another
No thinking about what you would rather
Buddha says focus stay clear
Present 365 days you have a year

Don't like what you have here
Things will not likely bring cheer
With clarity honor your essence
Maintain awareness celebrate presence

Can you center yourself in the present?
Can you observe your now while listening in service of yourself and others?

15 LOVES

Feeling inside warming cells
Footsteps lighter singing bells
Connections cure what's ailing
Magic of touch reframing

Many forms fill a sweet life
Parental romantic husband wife
Add to the list work you do
Inspiring motivating engaging too

Friendships glib and profound
Know importance when not around
Communities where you reside
Foster accomplishments and pride

Earth surrounds providing place
Potential of the human race
Bloodlines nurtured you then
When twilight you take care of them

These patches weave a cloth supreme
Clothe your life in a lovely dream
Don't be passive gifts wait for you
Make them happen all up to you

Where are you sated in love and what needs attention?
Do you acknowledge abundant blessings?

16 MOVING

Change starts deep inside
Preparing for a new ride
Bye to old hello new
Phasing out a usual hue

Been lost then found
Continuous go around
Through it before and again
All fine then however when

Think present not future/past
Weight will not last
Pulling toward guiding light
Vision on a fearful night

Deep knowing always here
Amid footsteps crying tears
Aware of that consciousness
Wisdom and loving kindness

Cross the chasm land like a feather
Suddenly no stormy weather
Mindful presence quiets concerns
Grow and change repeat the turns

What faith keeps moving you forward through changes and adversity?
Where do you turn in a crumbling and how does it help?

17 AWAKENED

New beginning
It's been a ninth inning
Stew in my juices
Center elusive

As one of the dancers
Search for answers
Balance this moment
Long last atonement

Path chosen no easy road
Took on a full bearing load
Living in conundrum
Better than humdrum

Life includes neurosis fear
Easy to fall hard on your rear
Tapes judgments bouncing brain
Truth lost at times in painful rain

Look out from your hole
Grab your vaulting pole
Did your best in this show
Now no place to go

Could quit and stop
Suck on a lollipop
Time to enjoy embrace who I am
An engaged committed authentic man

The last time you were "stuck" how did you let go of what was holding you?
How do you see your journey and can you help others who are stuck?

18 CONNECTION

Time now no other place
You can choose personal grace
Joy of life treat to humanity
Keeping us from insanity

Embrace rush to communion
Experience your sense of union
Stand with another I am here
Honor a pledge firm and clear

Trust the depth of your soul
Give yourself to a bigger whole
Honor the joy of sacred union
Why abandon joyous fusion

Pause on the edge of abyss
Let go of fear you cannot miss
Trust again honor your angels
No time to be strangers

Deepest learning here on earth
Increases all of your worth
When time for your end
Know you learned to bend

Therein strength of character
Fruit of life without barrier
Why wait what's the hesitation
Why delay connect for elation

Have you experienced the elation of union and communion?
Why resist joy, what are you waiting for?

19 COMFORT

You always belong home
Letting go not alone
Longing subsides no place to go
Feeling at ease peace you know

Warm essence when you arise
No conquest more than thrive
Caring for those you love
Joy communion blessed above

Resting easy breathing deep
Food delicious a long sleep
No need wander run hither yon
It's down home on your farm

Lonely tired stretched
In this comfort you can rest
What you need without asking
No longing purely basking

In this comforting space
Acknowledge who embodies grace
Remember they are here for you
Angels do what angels do

Do you have a comfortable place you thank people for making?
Can you make space a comfort for others?

20 BUSINESS

Busy-ness what it's about
Daycare a place to shout
Long lists filled with to do's
Creative arena many taboos

Place to engage competitive fire
Context for service that's higher
A ubiquitous social institution
For family religion a substitution

Expression of personal art
Platform for a fresh start
Exercises all parts of the brain
Creative edges in business terrain

For personal drama a great stage
Charm seduction competence rage
Theatre in which you learn
Realize dreams while you earn

Work occupies much of life
Your family sibling husband wife
Colleagues our trusted friends
Their satisfaction our ends

Is work a place to learn and collaborate or just to make money?
Do you see the workplace as an arena for service?

21 CHANGE

Static can rarely thrive
Change a sign of alive
Good to process until clear
Revelation shifts a gear

Complacent things remain
Egos resist new to sustain
Stars die cells rearrange
Holding on seems so strange

What does this teach and say
About voices seeking play
Hear answers in your soul
Teachers help on a roll

Trust messages and energy
Let a quest set you free
Return to familiar space
Circle your grounding place

Though it appears the same
Souls shift in failures shame
Ride currents navigate tide
Godhead counsel resides inside

How do you respond to change in your world?
What's your self-talk and resistance?

22 EDGES

Find strength in your weight
Remember sacred at every gate
No simple answers easy decisions
One foot then next endless revisions

Know joys that honor self
And the sadness heartsickness felt
Sitting on edge things unraveling
Voices at odds then a shattering

When young life was simple
Trauma an unwanted pimple
Older now know less and more
Complexity what we're here for

Not easier moving down your path
Tests increase need a nuanced craft
When pressure more than you can bear
A road beckons from over there

Back to your time in youth
Expect resolution in simplistic truth
Those days in the distant past
Allow solace of your private mass

What provides strength when feeling emotional and spiritual challenges?
What moves, nurtures and sustains you?

23 GROUND

Connections our source
In our moments no remorse
Present now attached alive
Like redwoods linked we thrive

Progress getting aligned
Connections front side behind
Mastery like fine wine
Grows as we rise and shine

Inside glory begins to emerge
Connections provide courageous nerve
Defining selves in relation to others
Sharing lives all sisters brothers

Enjoy the revelations profound
Joining others here on the ground
Close tight honor your dream
Engage loved ones they are supreme

Weather chasms of your soaring birth
Foster treasures here on earth
Enable best in you to emerge
Surrounding voices give life verve

What connections are you thankful for, what do they provide?
Who are you without them and what investment will you make?

24 CAPACITY

On sidelines observant wise
Plan critique heavy sighs
Fear what life demands
Take place in the band

Many lives lived being small
Never know how large their tall
Please engage at your pace
Find capacity and your grace

Sleep-walk day after day
Why not some raucous play
Never know who you might be
Act on the yearning and be free

Human beings live on earth
Blessed gifts come with birth
Potential of a larger plan
Realize as much as you can

Power to achieve noble goals
Beyond limitations told
Opportunity at your door
No more shyness go for more

What are the gifts you contribute to others?
How can you share more?

25 CLOUDS

Cloudy within and without
Flat haze no edge or shout
Summer wanes gone sun's kiss
Path gray muddy fading bliss

How to handle empty inside
No motivation for life's ride
Fear of what lies ahead
Want to lie low back to bed

Know you want much more
A life allowing you to soar
Be joyful within your time
Make sacred rhythm and rhyme

You decide darkness or delight
Choose to move without fright
Foggy horizon a dangerous view
Find your clear sailing that is true

Life is suffering Buddha said
We do to avoid moving instead
Know that it is so
Life follows where you go

Illusion and fog contain gifts
Demand a clear mental shift
Dwell on cloudy get into it deep
Choose diversion go back to sleep

Remember best way out is through
Let cloudy make friends with blue
Stay authentic in your core
Life the lesson you're here for

What clouds your life and how do you respond when gray arrives?
What value do clouds bring?

26 FAITH

Critical time for the human race
Thinking what happened to our grace
Call the wizards and magicians
Essential to be good tacticians

Need a clarified plan
Guide for woman children man
Leaders need context direction
No aspiration to perfection

Soul has capacity means
Ability to manifest dreams
Many unhappy folks think
I feel punk should be pink

Program to worship prosperity
Having more is the remedy
Won't make you happy or whole
Money's not care for soul

What force might rescue us
Help get off this careening bus
Let go of gold inspiration
Better gods for preservation

Manifest your plans and vision
As days unfold tailor revisions
Trust guides hear their voices
Ancient wisdom for your choices

Do you hear inner voices and listen to private guides?
Can you have faith in the wisdom of what they say?

27 FOOTSTEPS

Shed skins that tightly bind
Moving doors expanding find
Space bigger in your mind
Search for comfort of being kind

For some fixed routine
Others variety in their dream
Important know where's home
Though each juncture go alone

One step to the next rung
Quiet voices help the lunge
Not knowing a specific path
Wide narrow cut your swath

Make mistakes on your trail
At times forget your holy grail
One step then another
Cherish sister honor brother

Steps comfort your beast
Feeding hunger your new feast
Remember not them or you
Finding their way winners too

Pondering your next steps
God inside knows directs
First choose where then who
In that order to yourself be true

Remember what lights your path
Honor presence a heavenly bath
Always essential care for all
No reason in this world to fall

Where do you need to explore?
What are you searching for and what questions intrigue you?

28 CORRECTION

A blessing to find home
On a journey seeking whole
Perspective grows big tall
Wide perception learning for all

Mark beginnings of new life
Not hard to banish strife
Now it happens when you find
Healing for your mind

Engage your process make it fun
Never finished never done
Like a pilot NY to LA
Course corrections fill the day

Perfection longed for never found
Not a machine perfectly wound
Observe the journey up down
Find answers for your ground

Notice what sets you free
Be OK with who you be
Allow change growth pain
Remember rainbows after rain

Is life an unfolding never finished project or a destination to reach?
Can you accept where you are and forgive yourself for bumps of your journey?

29 MOTIVATION

Your horizon looks bleak
Closed throat can't speak
Where to go charge so low
Energy wanes no place to go

Longing incessant cup is dry
Looking up gray clouds the sky
Future a blank screen
Screaming inside feeling mean

Laughter smiles abandoned face
Life's work gone in disgrace
Loved ones can't help they try
Inside out wants to cry

Alarm says wake you say no
Nothing worthy where to go
Your get up got up and went
Your penny jar paid the rent

Place to turn inside you
Cells say time to renew
Continue to contribute presence
Drive to serve is your essence

Do you listen to the wisdom of your observer and not your monkey mind?
What happens when you don't pay attention to that inner voice?

30 ANSWERS

Cannot do without it
Inside quiet outside riot
Inner peace your ground
Makes wellness all around

Seek answers in self
Not anyone else
Oracles are never scared
Inner knowing not compared

When fearful fully embrace
Knowing sustains your grace
Your essence a prime resource
Rarely an external source

Let inner voices bubble up
That counsel fills your cup
Reflect on what is stored within
Allowing room for new whim

Answers to riddles of being
Unique solutions from clear seeing
Engage others hear them out
Final voice yours to shout

Do you seek others for your answers?
Can you transcend their thinking?

October

1 FAITH

Pulls us to the river of life
Brings elation joy strife
Doubt pervades your being
Courage fleeting hope receding

Pillar when you need a rock
Offers solace no matter the block
Not religion superior being
Bigger force expansive seeing

Meta to traditions of serenity
Force of life promise supremacy
Power within part of a plan
Food growing on magical land

All's OK trust it fits
Honor outcomes despite misfits
Each purposeful lesson a piece
Engage the game be released

Faith heals each day
Brings perspective in the fray
Get what you need for sure
No way out always a no door

Dreams fulfilled you have power
With you daily each minute hour
Trust goodness compassion each day
Honor what's you and play and play

Has doubt compromised and stopped you from trusting?
Given a choice why not believe dreams will manifest?

2 PASSAGES

Begin again renewed once more
Midnight's passage rough for sure
Tossing turning burning heart
Raging fire paused new start

Way we process musings internal
Night sweats terror fears eternal
Complex vehicle fine-tuned machine
Serving us nobly dream after dream

Wonder speculation needing whole
Dark passages moving your soul
As we traverse endless travails
Never sure why inquiry prevails

Not about conquest mountains seas
But mastering mind quieting disease
Journey of a conscious soul
Compassion acceptance filling your bowl

Imminent death was all I could see
Sharing myself with friends gracefully
Not all about dollars you reaped
Do those around enjoy peaceful sleep

Why are you here at this time?
What will fulfill your life purpose?

3 KNOWING

Vision cloudy concern for safety
Insecurity a sense of maybe
Not sure how future will unfold
Demons visit not secure or bold

Misgivings inside second guess
Life unravels a psychic mess
Work it through from your dream
Your angels as a go between

When disaster fills mind's eye
Lose reason sometimes start to cry
Place to resort a solid source
Always better than remorse

Grounding without fear
Security not sure from where
Heart's desire not crave or scare
Knowing next rung will appear

Trust voice inside sky above
Talk to yourself with love
Deliverance is guaranteed
Release demons breathe and breathe

Are you troubled by something real or old demons?
Have you grown since old conversations caused disturbance
and can you access current wisdom?

4 FACILITATION

Helping others here to there
Task we have why we're here
Draw out thinking as they reflect
Find places where they intersect

Discover what's in the way
Achieve goals they cannot say
Forge the groan zone nasty thick
Can't push hard or move too quick

Ground rules preventing fights
Sticking points and sleepless nights
What makes them trip and fall
What agreement satisfies all

Back in action engage a crusade
Use a toolbox so a craft is made
Heart-felt calling draws you to serve
At times though lose your nerve

Great satisfaction they're on track
Serve their mission turn your back
Next assignment in god's mind
Ignite vision passion in the blind

Frustration exhaustion at times unkind
Little time to breathe unwind
In moments feeling spent
Know your joy is heaven sent

*What satisfactions motivate you to serve others in connecting
and collaborating?*
Why do you pay the price!

5 ENOUGH

Stress strain seeking stature
Others notice that I matter
Want recognition sense of fame
Win at any cost a favored game

See accomplishments of others
Compete with sisters brothers
Take on this take on that
So they notice where I'm at

One day wake in wonder ask
Why do I do each lofty task
Don't have to do all that stuff
When I realize I am enough

I'm worthy deserving happiness
Not about doing but beingness
All honored goals and positions
Means little to real statisticians

Driven by mother father husband wife
Real question do I have a life
Happy is simple kind warm laughter
Gemutlich secure each day after

Prepare fresh food be close to earth
Smiling companions engender rebirth
Each deserves their bliss
You're enough for happiness

God gifted nature reflected in presence
Authentic expression emergent essence
The real gift you bring on earth
Essential you profound worth

What are you cultivating?
Will all the doing get what you want or is there a direct path?

6 BORN AGAIN

Handcuffs have me in chains
Afraid to move so much remains
Downward spiral free fall space
Never fit can't find grace

Limbs splayed braced for worst
In my throat unquenchable thirst
Terror surrounds little respite
No slumber can escape the fright

Eyes wide open slam the ground
Suddenly stopped quiet around
Silence surrounds still serene
Quiet arises from my dream

Held me gripped in a vise
Thoughts entrapped turned to ice
Longing missing open gash
Devastation caused the crash

If lucky fortune shines
Surrender and see your eyes
Let go of fixation's ride
Emerge on the other side

Through the tunnel light profuse
Wake discover your own truth
Journey each day in your mind
Choose a wise god to live inside

Do you know mood and perspective is a result of your thinking?
Are there places new thinking can provide rebirth?

7 SADNESS

Longing empty hole in heart
Saps intensity robs my art
Realize something's wrong
Flat-lined lost my song

Strange rhythm in my gait
Deliberate cadence embodies fate
Once joyous quiet sedate
Now missing a cherished mate

Footsteps hover near
Awaken knowing fear
Sadness kills rips apart
Tragedy of a broken heart

Stepping forward walk my path
Can't hide empty or a crash
Next trajectory to start
Reclaiming my joyous heart

Moving forward mindful clear
Accept sadness get beyond fear
Step into dark of being
Let learning reveal a song to sing

Feel the residual of your heartbreak?
Do you allow yourself the pain of loss and take lessons that serve you?

8 YOU

Deeply drawn together quickly pulled apart
Hole of separation completely empty heart
Breathing of another connected to a source
Life affirming texture quiets all remorse

Alone very quiet except for chattering mind
Reverie of oneness life of another kind
You are defined in culture and through others birthed
Human juxtaposition where we find our worth

Take a new found freedom feel it to the bone
Enjoy your aloneness though it's not your home
Find yourself in others let them fill your heart
As you react and interact discover your own art

Don't confuse the being that sits and meditates
With the personality choosing to relate
Gifts you bring to others take on many forms
Helping you discover edges of your norms

As your path continues one foot then another
Keep up relationships with sister and brother
Joy and satisfactions that you find in life
Discovered with others not locked in their strife

Engage be tenacious hold on don't let go
Find freedom in togetherness as you grow and grow
Others are your teachers others are your friends
Others are the treasures revealing your real ends

*Is your identity revealed by deciding or through discovery as you interact
with others?*
Do you closely engage with others and what is your identity in their minds?

9 LOYALTY

Meaning of a true heart
Giving heart heart that's smart
Solace to know somewhere
Other hearts for you are there

Critical lesson on our path
Heart connections quiet wrath
Relationships you count on
On your team some quickly gone

Making choices stop and ask
What implications from this task
Think long term not just tomorrow
Loyalty earned you cannot borrow

All around short-term relations
Not built on solid foundations
Connections deep in your heart
Money power not always smart

Treasure honored connections
ROI no short-term defections
Deposits in today's account
Pay dividends long term no doubt

Who's your team and what do you count on them for?
Do you thank them for long-term value they provide?

10 PARENTS

Source of essence place where formed
Learned habits beliefs observed norms
On a course with their set of things
Programmed before we grew wings

Gracious thanks we owe them
Without birthing we'd have no kin
As we get older awaken grow
We choose over decide our flow

They may resist our rebirthing
Not ready to bless our emerging
That's when resolve is tested honed
Building character for when alone

Love them anyway
Don't let resistance in the way
Fear is their holy cross
They would rather be boss

Can you love accept who they are
Honor their treasure though from afar
Thank acknowledge foundation they gave
Let your quest continue seek all you crave

Have you consciously chosen each value, ideal and goal you own?
How would new choices show up in your behavior and activities?

11 ORIGIN

Meaning of this word
Think warmth to absurd
Bosom longed for when away
Nest of freedom then you play

Home glowing embers warm hearts
Enraging inspiring motivating arts
Familiarity knows your presence
Heritage context of your essence

Blood relations origins genetic
Sometimes connections pathetic
Generating tumult strong emotions
Blurred boundaries magical notions

Preserving sacred traditions
Current grounding ancient religions
Visible place others see
Who is you who is me

Searching lost wandering spent
How to find where you went
Place to return hang with clan
Rest be held learn who you am

Who and what did family give you?
Do you return for their communion and have you forgiven them?

12 SELF MASTERY

Joyous deliverance engaging discovery
Healing communion souls touching lovingly
At times life reveals deeply
Hidden truths often so slippery

Go forth find your path
Longing touching a serenity bath
Comes from intimate discovery
Arising from connection recovery

On this journey of living
Searching hoping seek forgiving
A place to know being whole
As you find a permanent home

Communion joining others
Making them sisters brothers
Comes when one with self
Grounding that's real wealth

Find true self in others' reaction
Engage from authentic traction
Connect let go of any stealth
In the quest discover self

Do you self-disclose and share a real self?
What's the return and risk in being fully transparent?

13 CRADLE

Frightened shaken to the core
Concern end up on the floor
Recall foundation from youth
Warm cradle family sacred truth

Want a rich life experience
Achieve something serious
Giving taking ups downs
Support in many rounds

Uncles aunts cousins galore
Neighbors community to soar
Journey forth seeking life
Treasures loved cut with a knife

Concerned about rebirth
Searching for self-worth
Foundation connections in place
Family bosom opportunity grace

Did you find comfort and solace in family at challenging times?
Can you teach others how to be your best family?

14 RESPITE

Mother earth needs a rest
Preening birds say knowing best
Order clarity all know place
Thanksgiving for all in grace

Not always crystalized in glee
Need foundation peace harmony
Connect to others' cells slow down
Rest appreciation is the crown

Perspective is grounded serene
Life a dream state with no mean
That wealth engenders love
Start within see a dove

Lives inside human cells
Seated where center dwells
Though war often occupies life
Humanity does not need strife

Long for peace ongoing quiet
Rich insight a steady diet
Tranquil moments' sublime
Enjoy aspiration rest in time

How much of your life is lived in peace?
Do you value peace as aspiration with guidance for achieving it?

15 CONNECTION

Long for it constant search
Observe from a unique perch
Why we seek why we pray
Venturing out each day

Longing a place in the soul
Lack of chatter quiet whole
Connection to familial presence
Call it home feeds our essence

Supporting timbers stand us up
Belonging fills our cup
Core does not need much
Warmth familiar laughter and such

Alone lonely one car garage
Need a tribe to lift recharge
Sitting forlorn in our cups
What's missing valued much

Seeking ballast in your life
Resist stewing in your spice
Cross the chasm of inner space
Reaching others is your grace

What makes you feel centered and connected and what does it mean to you?
How do you access center and connection?

16 ANXIETY

Anxious nervous inside
Feeling helpless run hide
Sense of danger here before
Primal fear through that door

Essential discernments to make
Fear about now or an earlier take
What perspective do you choose
So fear is not perennial blues

When fear is welling inside
Do it anyway fear is a guide
Thank the fright a warning sign
Wake up pay attention to mind

Warning from a historic past
Primitive guard helped you last
Feelings not all about now
In the body reflect slow down

Fear an ally welcome an old friend
Demanding attention for the next bend
Learn to trust fear is a tool
Honor it manage it suffer no fool

What are you fearing now?
Can you treat fear as ally and friend helping you achieve a desired end?

17 LANDED

Many spend years locked in mind
Inside a body where you reside
Year upon year marching through time
Busy about in the midst of fine wine

Worry this worry that
Mindless chatter chat chat chat chat
Living in heads buzzing about
One day body calls with a shout

Illness accident injury
Can you pause to find a me
You're more than thoughts reactions
More than emotions attractions

Finally quiet whole self at peace
Let go with a sense of release
Whatever fears from your past
Awareness transcends them at last

From the belly of your machine
Deeper life force manifests a dream
Sense yourself walking on holy turf
Finally landed on solid earth

Embrace terrain though it feels strange
Requires your life to rearrange
Enjoy the comfort serenity brings
God stands within all sentient beings

If you were walking on new ground what would it feel, look, smell taste like?
Are others served by your change of presence?

18 PASSAGE

What's your happiness and delight
Makes you smile middle of night
Tickles your sweet heart
Generates the quickening of art

Ensures you're not alone
Laughter far from home
Joyful reminder you're god's child
No matter distance no matter how wild

You have an enduring state
Place to return starting gate
Sustains you each dark night
Finding that peace your greatest fight

Life on earth bump and grind
Treatment often so unkind
Abide knowing what you came for
Lessons embodied in each door

Rarely about what happens to us
Achievements please do not fuss
Being centered grounded clear
Experience is why you're here

Learning knowing makes you smile
Only here for a small while
Honor companions in whom you delight
On passages from dark to light

What learning generates wisdom and pleasure for you?
Do you acknowledge the joy that brings?

19 OTHERS

What's your ultimate vision
What you see with precision
Evaluate things you do
Do they bring happiness to you

What gives meaning to your quest
Where you decide what is best
Have you reached your all
Counted among those standing tall

As we advance in age
Life force transforms rage
From focus on me me me
We look outward see a thee

Fortunate marching along
Shift perspective change the song
From focus on what we earn
The gift becomes what we learn

Count blessings end of day
Measure others state of play
Those who you care and give
Measure life by how they live

What's the life of those you hold dear?
Have you affected them in meaningful ways?

20 RECIPROCITY

Birth cradle feed till contented
Without them needs unattended
More than physical they provide
Instill well-being confidence pride

Foundation essential to being
Grounding and encourage seeing
Education finances too
Clothe bodies give each foot a shoe

Fortunate their work doesn't quit
No matter age count on their grit
Never abandon responsibility
Well of giving sets you free

Cycle reverses at some time
Become caretaker without a whine
Solid footsteps covered ground
Now they're slowing down

Give back what you took for granted
Their giving got you firmly planted
Magic happens something like that
As you give get so much back

Many lessons from their being
Experience of living and seeing
Cycle of life revolving door
Giving taking what you came for

Who parented you and where are you in the cycle?
Can you acknowledge gifts received and honor reciprocity?

21 CHOICES

Life is choice bounty surrounds
Savor flavors found all around
Glitter's attractive also meat
What you engage all a big treat

Riches present sometimes disguised
Capture the dreams in visions eyes
Mindfulness serves making all real
Provides awareness of how you feel

Glory present deep in eyes
Also in hearts filling blue skies
Mirrors reveal what you have sown
Through illusions get closer to bone

Reflect on choices you make
Careful of fantasies turning out fake
Be aware of illusion trust god inside
Steadfast vision your clear sight guide

Indecision a weakening sign
With clarity guiding all works out fine
Ask get answers listen carefully
In fright hours honor all you see

Are you pleased with what's around you reflecting the sum of your choices?
What choices enable what you want today?

22 GRIEF

Profound sadness part of me died
Innocence shattered inner child cried
Everyday taken I was given tears
Forsaken by a god of many years

Compass spinning lost control
Emotions gyrate in an empty hole
Feeling anger desire to attack
Heart knows it's not going back

Endure sadness mourn what's gone
Realize the missing shocked awake at dawn
Can't shorten grieving pretend what's not so
Palliatives can't help ignore the huge blow

Get down in anger feel burning rage
Aching heart lion pacing its cage
Within searing heartache anguish pain
Sunny expectations now dark clouds rain

Sit with sadness know what's missing
Be still feel pain in the reminiscing
Wisdom more powerful than a shove
Victory is knowledge with resolve

Reflect on behavior causing a lash out
What needs forgiving let humanity out
Let go of enemy let love fill your heart
Not truly forsaken just shown another part

Mortal players on god's living stage
Learning lessons of wisdom love rage
Let go the isolation of the cavernous I
Choose to be connected under sacred sky

End of the journey we choose going home
Or come back again if stuff you won't own
Take messages heard way deep inside
Honor all voices OK have some pride

You a blessed temple noble house erect
Caution the meddling of those you respect
Be brave honor your eternal truth
Stop any hiding go behind feigning youth

You are a perspective another voice of god
With so many others in each precious pod
Bless your earth experience respect others' too
No winners or losers that's an old taboo

Enjoy all your freedom frolic on stage
Shun repressive forces they never engage
End a beginning something fresh and new
Suffering pain of grief the way out is through

What is the crucible containing your biggest lessons?
Who would you be without them and are you grateful for the wisdom?

23 TERROR

Many sizes shapes and forms
Righteous in their truth and norms
Their way the only path
Zealotry spewing fear and wrath

Always make presence felt
Claims of being heaven sent
Other's evil justifies harming
Never dialogue or warning

Why create fear in others
Terrorize sisters brothers
Striking innocents selfish snakes
No consequence as they forsake

Do you react to strike burn
Or slow the other cheek and turn
Time provides a course to take
Vengeful thoughts leave a wake

Actions taken without seeing
Have a twisted way of being
Lesson here to take away
Change your life day to day

Let presence be simple clean
Human bearing project a dream
Get along without hating them
Model embody admired then

Sleep softly let presence be felt
Smile quietly in silence to self
Fierce clear in what you came for
Never pride at heaven's door

Any terrorists holding you hostage?
Do you hold others hostage?

24 SOFTEN

Opening up letting go
Softening heart lets you grow
Embrace others with compassion
Solid platform with more traction

No gnarling white knuckle fist
Suddenly life has a new twist
More choices at your feet
Renewal snatched from defeat

Positions trap your being
Rigidity blocks clear seeing
Now the time for you begin
Give yourself a big wide grin

Let right vanish from your heart
Melt barricades keeping you apart
We all choose happy or right
One imprisons one takes flight

As you go as you grow
A blessing you need to know
Give the love longed for self
It returns from everyone else

Do belief systems diminish your capacity to connect and sustain relationships?
Are they moral imperatives or choices?

25 CARESSING

In service poised with a mission
Honorable purpose awaits commission
Years spent hoping to get
Leave you in an empty fret

Big trick to living quite simple
Giving to all creates a dimple
No sitting gloomy deep agitation
Instead generate great expectation

Landscape reveals places that need
Giving mode eliminates greed
What you get shock surprise
More than seeing with your eyes

Built into your biological machine
Hands caress wipe tears clean
Your nature wants to take care
Compassion gives back so dare

Don't wait for others to care for you
Find places to give jump into the stew
Give freely do not hide gifts inside
They heal and bless and foster pride

How does it feel to reach and give to others?
What do you get from giving and where are people who can use what you have?

26 RAGE

Buried deep a primal scream
From injustice we have seen
Dormant til awakened
Lines crossed innocence taken

Welling up from forsake
Piercing shriek pulsating wake
Essence of this primal call
Suffering from a fall

Rage in collective memory
Souls trampled in history
Powerful charge profound
Past present future ground

What can you engage
To quell aggression of this rage
Violence makes things worse
Lashing magnifies the curse

Can you take the path of love
Can you coo like a dove
Forgive let compassion flow
Let horror end choose let go

What triggers your rage and how do you get through it?
What have you learned for the next time?

27 MELANCHOLY

Heartaches of the soul
Missing what made you whole
Part of essence filling you
Absent you feel blue

Many never find or know
Treasured blessings of loving so
Once you taste a sacred kiss
All is scant to that bliss

Lonely ache creeps in
Reminds you left on a whim
Let go wisdom tempted fate
Rearranged a stable state

Lovely path you had set
Topsy-turvy in unrest
Something good pure at source
Turned asunder to divorce

Knowing what you know now
Foundation served you somehow
Reflecting a lifetime later
Might have been so much greater

Answers buried deep inside
Apology can't erase ego's pride
No choice so you let go
Now know the hurt you did sow

What part of past are you holding that it's time to let go?
What purpose does it serve and what's the payoff?

28 ACCEPTANCE

Vision we have for our path
Others can't see maybe they laugh
Pictures differ do not intersect
So we draw back protect

Not knowing what they think
No clear speaking or link
Without place without voice
Leaving you without choice

Long to belong a place of home
Find right space not alone
Search earnestly follow your nose
At times thorns at times rose

Essential practice for success
Being kind yields happiness
Onward on your tack
Honor others have their back

Core of your humanity
Nurturing eyes that see
Honor vision from inside
Do no harm simply glide

Why pretend a connection is compatible when not?
What cost learning what to do differently?

29 PERSPECTIVE

Choices to choose
Choices say win lose
How we frame questions we ask
Determines how we see a task

Music to dance sounds in our head
Conductors control what's said
Way we hold things says soar or fall
It's not random at all

Smart knows what to do in the whirl
Brilliance what to think in the swirl
How we approach perspective we create
Determines outlook dismal or great

Path we act out on this earthly plane
Marks our existence and what remains
Make choices when awake
Shape the life you get to create

Remember you have control
Determine how you grow old
Mindful aware of cause and effect
Perspective promotes your happiness

Glass half empty or half full - how has
your perspective been shaped by confirming or disconfirming events?
What is the impact of perspectives in your current reality?

30 CENTERING

Unbalanced dizzy crazed
Cells need to be rearranged
What intervention is fast
What path grounding at last

Family bloodline genes
Chemicals drugs food as wings
A dear one a lover friend
Art takes you round the bend

Nature leads back to your path
Womb water of a ritual bath
What these vehicles do
Align cells in the core of you

React to falling off your train
Here again in this pouring rain
Reframe opportunity welcome the fall
Downpour a path to more of your all

Mistake seeking answers out there
Always head back to your lair
Rain sunshine joy pain
Signposts get you home again

What do you do when off center to get back on track?
How does funk serve you?

31 FEAR

Grabs pulls your heart
Quiets creativity stifles art
Not knowing what lies ahead
No celebrating sense of dread

Imperceptible on your screen
Source of discomfort not seen
Its' presence impacts your life
Powerful emotion causing strife

Core of discomfort and pain
Process bringing rain
Gripped tightly by fear
Holds you back now next year

Answer simple the cure too
Fear future afraid of new
Unknown effects of a new act
Locks you up says no new tack

The cure faith trust in self
Your footsteps good as anyone else
Trust guides to lead you home
Trust the sacred never alone

Trust each step you take
Master guides moves you make
Venturing forth on your path
Angels guide you in a sweet air bath

What holds you back from pursuing longings?
Might life be different if you go beyond the fear of new and changing?

November

1 KNOWING

Yes or no pondering next
Stewing this that not know what's best
Seeing right wrong assessing blame
Mulling details righteous or shame

Amazing mind scan judges a scene
Quickly good bad rank in between
Sometimes trapped thinking we know
Looking for answers that satisfy so

Does not work that way at core
We rationalize what we stand for
Understand you get to choose
Wrong mindset will help you lose

Little truth or objective measurement
Say black white foment argument
Each finds what they believe
Courageously reject each other's sieve

Go along accept ways of being
Follow herd-mind killing your seeing
Aging you choose or slowly die
Decide the time to go home to your sky

How have choices contributed to you and what have you learned
about choosing?
Do you have situations that require new choices?

2 AFTERMATH

Now the time here the place
Begin to act from grace
Battle joined action noble
Fighting only generates trouble

Breach created by push or shove
Then we show what we're made of
Character that's truly real
Display how to teach and heal

Fierce fight on the wire
No winner or one to retire
Combat in venues changing
Players thinking rearranging

Can we learn from winter's night
Can body politic cease to fight
Energy wasted silly fray
Better spent another way

Winner loser an old frame
How about a bigger game
Perhaps sacred collaborations
A new pulse for great nations

We have tools technology
Let's aspire to real democracy
Time to move in this direction
Let others watch and pay attention

Do you interact with political views different from yours?
What might you learn with curiosity and empathy?

3 HOMEWARD

Grounded center runs deep
Important on a path so steep
Available though many layers
Resistance from many players

Perilous trail switchbacks dead ends
Erratic shifts many bends
False starts distractions injuries too
Furious activity nothing to do

Faith fuels the voyage home
Deep within never alone
Feeling lost without hope
Deeply embedded gyroscope

How to know you arrived
Beckoning from inside
Servants draw sacred bath
Reveal a more challenging path

No end this life or next
Epic story unending text
Journey home discovery birth
Transforming misery to mirth

Learn accept thankfulness too
Borrowed vehicles teaching you
Allow partners of spirits inside
Walk with god you've arrived

Is your journey a learning lesson or ongoing drama?
Can you focus on lessons for the bigger goal?

4 BOOMERANG

Quality honored thirsted for
Through life we want more
Others' blessings close at hand
Enabling joy part of a band

People you count on always there
Comforting guiding wiping a tear
Cajoling when you don't make sense
Nearer to you than anyone else

Through storms sunshine rain
Navigating all terrain
Back seat driving a positive presence
Whatever challenge giving essence

Unspoken promise be what you need
All circumstance they come to feed
Net worth includes value of friends
Comrades helping achieve your ends

Attract their gifts to your path
They are your healing bath
Easy simple child's play
Get all you want give all away

How do you give and serve those that need? Is there
a cost and what is the value to them and you?

5 BOLDNESS

No wasting time today
No dress rehearsal for the fray
No whimpering indecision
No time for revision

Greatness is within you
Trust faith let it through
Learn to love your shout
There inside let it out

Messages to deliver
No fear be a giver
Gifts now not tomorrow
Find a way beg steal borrow

Join others in healthy union
Mission bathed in communion
Stand tall with those beside
Trust conscience will guide

Glory here in engagement
Make sure to arrange it
The mission part of a plan
To uplift the human clan

How do you deliver full value of your gifts?
Who is needed on your team?

6 TRANSITIONS

Gliding on buoyant air
Thankful for being here
Lovely feelings for current flight
Friends bridged darkest night

Moves on changes shifts on shifts
Sometimes great emotional fits
Shaken core filled with fright
Knew transition was so right

Pure joy across the room
Even when night is noon
Time for movement and a shove
Always holding onto love

Glory on the other side
Each next step adds to pride
Mindful essence is the core
Reflecting what you came for

Others mirror and feedback
Wisdom keeps you on track
While soaring on feathery wings
Hold onto love in earnest cling

What or who keeps you grounded?
How does their presence contribute to the structure and fabric of your life?

7 CONTEXT

I live in this time and place
I try to embody grace
Journey at times tumultuous painful
End result gainful and grateful

Alive in a body we're here for
Make our days count for more
On earth more than accumulation
Can we find lasting elation

Things have value and they call
Don't meet deeper needs expect a fall
Take care of business free your mind
Beyond what it is you long to find

Inner journey what life's about
Reveal the power of your shout
External experience provides context
Don't fool yourself in material excess

How to shape what you do
Ask your heart to tell you
Don't give in to doubt or fear
Honor the grace of being here

What context does the voice of your heart provide?
How often do you listen and what calls your attention?

8 DYING

On your path of living
Slow to a sense of forgiving
Forgive this let go that
Moving on the jagged track

Not easy gets more complicated
Moving along sometimes belated
Clarity comes after the fact
Understanding after the act

Tricks a simple mind plays
Navigating counting days
Not forever here on earth
Begin dying time of birth

Happens at a point in time
Body fails we lose brine
Muscles weaken hearts flutter
Speech slurred eloquent stutter

Days numbered bodies thick
We reflect gone by too quick
Thinking back on youthful reign
Happy often laced with pain

Endure focus on joy in place
Footholds on the path to grace
Applause not what to expect
Always giving salves regret

Do you hold past betrayals leaving residual poison?
Do you know forgiveness is a gift to yourself?

9 MARRIAGE

Special promise connection love
Blessed by an elegant dove
Sharing joy emotion pain
In friendship sunshine rain

Sacred connection inner source
Deeply bonded cannot divorce
Living together year after year
Character generated here

Comfort of presence each bestows
Provides context everyone grows
Solid foundation called home
Place you step into rarely alone

Joy of communion celebration faith
Puts you through paces out of the gate
Experience in which you learn
Reveals essence and beauty of burn

Not taken lightly or profane
Jagged edges will chase you in pain
Take from its hearth wise and warm
Fills your being as each day you're born

Have you experienced sacred union in life?
What have been the benefits, challenges, learnings?

10 CARETAKING

A truth in living
Need caretaking forgiving
Someone salving ills
When cold warming chills

No matter how successful rich
Sentient life can be a bitch
Look for balance peace serenity
Centered in being sets you free

Search for ground you call home
Authenticity to caresses your moan
Quiet yearning fills what's missing
Provide a solace a face for kissing

Going forward growing up
Realize you get filling them up
Longed for a place to glow within
Be generous with your sweet grin

Are you in a caretaking circle?
Who do you comfort and who do you get comfort from?

11 LEAVES

Brilliant fire leaves in trees
Shimmering colors weaken knees
Days shorter chill fills air
Spirits quiet winter near

Fall when energy wanes
Hibernation frost on panes
Getting older wiser so
Being begins letting go

Dormant seedlings all around
Soft voices in frozen ground
Energy shifts no sign of spring
Perspective here quiets our sing

Black ice of a winter storm
Faith of heart to be reborn
Spring after silence enough
Around the corner of gray stuff

Deeper wisdom emerges
Chatter inside purges
Hunker down close to core
Clarity what you came for

Is there a deeper purpose in your life
to might discover in the respite of winter?
What might you make more available to
self and others?

12 SERVICE

Great joy generating peace
Serving another provides release
Move from thoughts of self
Compassion for someone else

Mothers for infants a given
Hospice more than a living
Let go of one's needs
Forget personal greeds

Stand in shoes of a person down
Embrace concerns never frown
Empathy a primary driver
A different modern-day striver

Quiet reverie not a priority
Don't think just do and be
Some learn at an early age
Giving develops your sage

Simply true on earth
Service quickens rebirth
No sitting focused on self
Simple ask who needs help

Can you focus on others needs and look for where you can you serve?

13 OLD SOULS

What is a pure human being
A soul well-traveled and well seeing
Young souls wrestle fuss fight
Old softer souls have earned insight

They know their journey home
Old souls are close to bone
Wise perspective is their art
A life evolved head to heart

They understand nourishing food
Essential for a fine mood
Not winning or earning status
Growing learning service matters

Lose direction stressful life
Visit a mindful older midwife
Find an old soul sit at their feet
Drink in dignity enjoy the treat

Have faith in lessons they hold
Heed their direction on the road
Angels among us god's message intact
Follow their footsteps for the right tack

Do you know an old soul?
What do you observe, what value do they provide?

14 REAL

Body tight back spasms back
Screaming inside feeling attack
Freeze in terror startle to stone
Naked truth you are alone

Notice aggression taking your hand
You want to fight so take a stand
Steeling yourself girded like rock
Inside ticking tightly wound clock

Realize the tension is you
Not letting go of things to do
Try giving up not doing more
Forgive and not be so sure

Accept happenings in life
Traversing cycles serene strife
Recognize you're not always alone
Forces inside carry you home

Fearful filled with tears and rage
Turn to counsel a noted sage
Look to heart spirit inside
Faith wisdom trust honor pride

Resist comparing your path
Be unique in your private bath
Trust personal lessons that reveal
Journey where you are most real

Feel incomplete or inadequate?
Can you hear self-talk and feelings and let go of actions based on old programs?

15 CANCER

Cell growth with its own mind
Dividing at will being wild
Most cells follow a plan and time
Invasive cancer its own rhyme

What's the origin of this demon
Terrorizing so many men and women
Sometimes genetic sometimes air
No right wrong or what's fair

Hit with chronic disease
Throws you to your knees
Treatment awful expense huge
Can't predict win or lose

Scrounge no regard for age or race
Compassion required for your place
Lessons for all in the sphere
Teaching mostly school of fear

No matter how big you are
Stricken by a common bar
In the circle of this powerful force
Cancer a teacher without remorse

What is your capacity for resilience?
How have you learned from challenges and how do the lessons enhance your
life today?

16 GUILT

Powerful emotion driving action
Impacts behavior dilutes traction
Longing forgiveness release of pain
Searching for sunshine in pouring rain

What are you guilty about
Response awakens with a shout
Blame shapes moves compromises fame
Your life controlled by shame

How can you quiet guilt
Feel better about your quilt
Keeps you from fully realizing self
Holds you back from deserved wealth

Is your life under disguise
Does shrouding keep you alive
Repeating a nightmare dream
Is not pretty or squeaky clean

Can you break the chain of prison
Quiet guilt with revision
Let go of guilt don't feel so bad
Enjoy the life that's yours to have

What are the places where guilt is a driver in your life?
If you change that how would your life be different?

17 COMMUNITY

Search to satisfy longing
Place we rest in belonging
Let down quiet all cells
Beneath personality our real selves

Place to plug in center source
Waters flow to chart a new course
Grounding our electrical rain
Comfort simplicity no chattering brain

Familiar faces our home
Conversation connection beyond alone
Restful sleep heals to the bone
Nourishment feeds existential moan

When you get restless in your wake
Can't find traction enabling a brake
Feelings induce tranquil sleep
Words of Jesus hit very deep

Remember a suggested answer
Plug into a place stop disaster
Two or more gather as one
Community connection a shining sun

Where do you plug in, rest deeply and feel home?
Have you thanked people in that space, acknowledging what they provide?

18 CLEAVING

Never easy leaving a lover
Pulling apart from sacred other
Leaving sweetness bonding brings
Alone again after heart sings

Back to separate of alone
No more cocoon shared in clone
Leaving cleaving heaving behind
Limitations of only one mind

Return to heart space of one
Familiar though not nearly as fun
Focus who might be next
In the meantime often pretext

No need reason or plan
Longing heart of woman or man
Joyous unions congeal mind
Leave part of self behind

Empty feeling lesser spark
Affirm connection no simple lark
No more important activity found
Deeply connected in sacred ground

Cherish love and gifts of communion
Honor sweet voice of union
Covet with reverence quickening hearts
Enable that presence wherever it starts

Trust aliveness and joy it brings
Bathe in beauty soar over things
Never lose sight the gift and blessing
Sweet love part of your questing

As life wanes one thing to know
Every love flight caused you to grow
At the end one thing you have
Memories of love the sweetest salve

What have you learned from love connections?
How have they contributed to you and do you give them recognition?

19 CARETAKING

Happy in a world gone insane
Form of connecting lessens all pain
In the midst of conflict and strife
Keeps you from leaving this life

Dear ones happy anxiety gone
Childhood illusions left back on the farm
Pursuing frivolity no longer cool
Though we linger a bit as yesterday's fool

Happy a moment dot on a line
Smile bursts forth a blip in time
Place of connection tickles your heart
Like the purity conveyed in art

Life mission makes you whole
Steadfast perseverance of a noble goal
Working toward a sweet end
Friendships on which you depend

The real gift seeing and giving
Engender laughter foster believing
Hearing those stuck in druthers
Inducing joy in heart mind of others

Don't worry what you have to do or be
That is the presence of your small me
About filling all those you can
Work uplifting the family of man

*Are your actions guided by contributions
you make to others? Are you maximizing
your gifts and the value they provide?*

20 BELONGING

Comfort in body stillness of soul
Safety close to home
Respite from buzzing around
Manic in search of quiet ground

Aside from what you came to do
You long for a quiet true
You're accepted can really be
Not what you do to find a real me

Deliverance sets you free
Grounded focused how you be
For the lucky good fortune shines
Comfort of quiet minds

Your own acceptance a powerful gift
Quiet inside without any rift
In this solid place sing your own song
Your heart revealed where you belong

Fully seen feeling so clean
Discovering your unique human being
Fortunate you can taste the honey
The sacred worth more than any money

How do you know you are home?
When you go how long do you stay and what has you leave?

21 WISDOM

Present here flowing serene
Calming focused white light beam
Value brought very strong
Realization before too long

Expanding life work abounds
Structure adds to the profound
On the verge of partnership
Generating an emerging blip

Ready willing push from my end
At times not the greatest friend
Forced production causes stress
Sometimes induces restlessness

Good news I can reach the shore
Letting go of armor allows for more
With the struggle of push and strive
Don't know how I've stayed alive

Heart knows no place else to go
Smarter than head what a pro
An organ for next generation
Big body pump no hesitation

Look for what is next
Forty years doing my best
Not going out with flames aglow
Quietly shared what I know

Do you look for real wisdom in the head or heart?
What's the difference and why do you trust one or the other?

22 TRANSMUTING

Numb not fully present
Anger disappointment resentment
Knowing what's not right
Loving I won't have tonight

Seeking from deep anger
Richer longer truer stronger
Disappointment sends you reeling
Beneath the rage sad cauldron of feeling

Future envisioned sweetest kissing
Vision had mostly missing
Not what you thought you had
Wide chasm makes you sad

How to cure fix heal
First acknowledge accept reveal
Gentle salve the caress of love
In time declare you've risen above

Let it instruct teach its' lessons
Learnings are treasured possessions
The experience guides self and others
Share wisdom with sisters brothers

Transmute suffering for all you can
God's way of teaching a bigger plan
Adopt perspective not all about you
Learning helps carry us through

Embrace what I'm talking about
Awakened smiles replacing pout
See value in the gift of knowing
Foster wisdom teaching growing

How have you used lessons from sadness and disappointment for self and others?

23 RELEASE

Life takes us places
Where we never expected graces
Often surprising counter intuitive
Locations for varietal renewing

Learn the feel of life's tether
Loving this and that together
As we age if we're smart
Honor passages of the heart

Honest about self
No hating someone else
Don't dislike who they are
Just reject actions ajar

Reflect on your dis-ease
Clear about what would please
We have choice how we react
Hold your anger use your tact

When deeply hurt just forgive
Noble path the way to live
Let go scorn continue love
Mindful connect godhead above

Can you choose more compassion toward others?
Do you know forgiveness takes care of self by letting go of anger more than
releasing another?

24 THANKSGIVING

Give thanks this time of year
For freedom fortune good cheer
Stomachs full in safe houses
Art and passion that arouses

Families sacred presence
Lovers who give their essence
Acknowledge and appreciate
Abundance fills your plate

Warm season time for reflection
Stay conscious check direction
Recline enjoy repast
Material comforts easily crash

Look at news so much trouble
Tinderbox to burst your bubble
Incendiary spots need your skills
Many suffer cure their ills

Give thanks for what you bring
Give to make others sing
Acknowledge honor share
Care for souls thin and bare

What blessings are you thankful for?
Does inner dialogue prevent fully appreciating yourself and others?

25 WATERS

Waters deeper than you know
Wellspring depth you can go
Blooming exploding uncapped
Waiting dormant until tapped

Conscious of what's stored inside
Thoughtful access without pride
Gifts given from tools you hold
Wisdom to share many fold

Dreaming pondering a move
Steps without a need to prove
What's missing you can fill
Voice for voiceless use your will

Inquiry discovery leveraging self
Talents serving everyone else
Not in places obvious
Risky spaces more perilous

Keep living answer the phone
Rest in assurance you're not alone
From deep places near your core
Pathways to what you came for

Have you discovered strengths deep in you?
How do you use and teach others?

26 DIVERSITY

The word demands a context
What's it mean what steps next
Programs atoning for the past
Evoking what we know can't last

Affirmative action quotas and such
Discrimination lawsuits crush
Labeling formulas engendering fear
What moves get us there from here

Beyond threats and bluster
About growth to muster
Tolerance openness seeing others
Aspiration for sisters brothers

Key to victory deliverance
Stop the focus on difference
Superficial diversions
Call up pointless aspersions

Recognize we're much the same
Let black white red yellow fade
World shifts dominance reverses
See the truth beyond old curses

Way to success feeling clean
Let go divisions that are mean
Realize what you've been told
Stories not truth let go they're old

Where do you harbor bigotry and does it serve or hurt?
What will deliver inclusion and belonging?

27 DISILLUSIONMENT

Trusted icons institutions that inspire
Ideas ideals lighting your fire
Concepts constructs held in heart
Principles you count on history art

Shock your system far wide deep
Perspectives making you weep
Inside sadness rage disbelief
Innocence shattered engaging grief

Living moving through daze
Bedrocks relied on shifting to haze
Foundation shaken can't speak a sound
Profound confusion seeking new ground

Once confident on bedrock
Solid support reliable clock
Now sandcastles all's disappeared
Realize just what you feared

Pushing limits testing bounds
Undoing of self searching next rounds
Vista focus frames what you see
All before you choose carefully

What individual or institution has disappointed you?
Do you devote time for discernment on the edges?

28 COMPLETION

Time for saying good-bye
Yesterday's joy makes you cry
Tears laughter left behind
Remembering yesterday's child

Goodbye not easy often rough
Experience profound never enough
Another's presence warmth they bring
Memories tattooed when hearts sing

When time tie loose ends
Completion before new friends
May not be pretty or nice
Adults make choices sacrifice

Remember as you toss and turn
No matter this that always learn
Never despair forks in the road
Whatever direction carry the load

Choose wisely know significance
Whatever you do has consequence
Your process shows the way
Always completion perhaps not today

How do you say good-bye to people, places, projects needing completion?
How do you care for self and others in transition?

29 ALONE

Born and die alone here in between
Most of alone hardly ever seen
Engage others one form or another
Live communally with sisters and brothers

With others we find self
Defined by everyone else
Most in communion at home and work
Choosing alone a special quirk

Unique reason to choose alone
No solace in a family home
Outsiders artists monks and mystics
Observe others keep their statistics

Different lives different game
Sometimes alone achieves great fame
Ask icons if they are alone
Their craft seems to be their home

Operate beyond fortune fame
Need for others no cause for pain
Rejoice connection with family friends
Celebrate heal those needing mends

Cherish good fortune love sing praise
Honor connections of familial ways
In the end all are alone
Enjoying the abyss of sacred unknown

Who makes up your community and how do they define and contribute to your life?
Do you acknowledge and thank them enough?

30 COMPANIONSHIP

Feline creatures slither about
Under foot block any route
Sashaying all over the room
Feeling low they lift gloom

Sweet things curled in your lap
Sandpaper tongue venus fly trap
Beautiful eyes staring agape
Mystery in your landscape

Stalking big ones rule the day
Jumping chasing subduing prey
Fleet afoot rocketing around
Beautiful coats patterns astound

A source of companionship
Solace when you have a blip
Of pure independent means
Obeying not in their genes

Wonderful beasts serving well
A few around make life swell
Looking for respite retreat
Commune with cats under your feet

Do you find cats fun, engaging, curious, entertaining, humorous, diverting,
helpful, healing?
Do you know why?

December

1 PEACE PRAYER

Pray for a longing inside
Demands attention disturbs pride
Thorn that won't go away
Needles serenity says no to play

Not rest till thrown down
Replaced a smile with a frown
Pollutes air water you drink
Cloudy judgments needing a shrink

Rage inside breaks a sweet heart
Prowls deep corridors demanding art
Shocks your wisdom drawing tears
Grows louder each passing year

Curdling screams from your chest
Calls your voice to rise up protest
Galvanizes burning within
Occasionally restores a grin

Amazed at what you observe
Crazyness ignites each nerve
Postpone life wanting more play
You're alone with much to say

One answer wells up in being
World is peaceful people seeing
Tend to suffering heal all ills
Loving kindness of clear wills

Realize violence only gets more
Know love is what we came for
Let go all thoughts of winning or blame
Let go all war with it our shame

Honor peaceful compassion we are
Let go what won't take us far
Singing clear voices angels we are
Let go dis ease that won't take us far

What can you let go of to serve broader peace? Can you forgive and let go of suffering now?

2 SERENITY

Stop searching for goals
Stop baffling on shoals
Striving won't take you where
You are already there

Nothing there no place to go
Realize you just don't know
Presence questing to reach
Nothing you can't already teach

Serenity is inside you
Embrace nothing to do
No action just letting go
Listen inside from that grow

Peace in accepting what's so
Trust your process to know
Ego always needs more
Live moments you're here for

You are already whole
Rich fertile never alone
Deep quiet in your soul
Nourish in your mixing bowl

Is habitual striving blocking peace and serenity?
Can you embrace your wholeness?

3 DOUBT

Careful of voices that question you
Often chatter monkey minds pursue
Mindless words they are from
Sources can make you numb

Meek souls complacent at best
Rarely challenge no self-conquest
Bold want something more
Courage in what they're here for

Pulled by visions gleam
Hearing voices of their dream
At times a whisper or a shout
Vigilance managing their pout

Frightened voices in your brain
Say cancel cancel no time for rain
Acknowledge cautions' thoughtful voice
Mindfully respond solidify choice

This process serves your desires
Grounding fantasies pure heart aspires
Thank provocations causing chagrin
Providing guidance from within

Pursuing personal mission what do you tell yourself about why or not the path is worthy?
How do you get beyond excuses to your life's work?

4 SERVING

Living learning to serve
Let go ego grow more nerve
Shift focus I to thou
Care for others then now

Life of service simple not hard
Let go I focus look out at the yard
Who wants to get where
Encourage steps sit back cheer

Glory of this precious art
Wells inside fill your heart
Shifting gaze inside to out
Helping others to their stout

New habits opposite to
Cultural learning all about you
Hell's a place locked inside
I focus only no cause for pride

Guide yourself a step at a time
Sharing caring life is sublime
Connect to your giving source
Actualize without remorse

Is your focus on self or others?
What focus would satisfy both yourself and others?

5 BLISS

Holds you demands attention
Charts your life sets direction
Grounds gives days meaning
Answers to your screaming

Are you drifting and pretending
Do you have a force compelling
Channels energy focuses intention
Sets priorities demands reinvention

In your life look for times
Everything perfect rhymes
Fully engaged to a demand
Perspective clear even-hand

Draw from that blissful state
You your action all else can wait
Lost your essence then you find
The sense of being left behind

Gift of bliss waits for you
Clear voices tell what to do
Reveal and thrill you with joy
Remind you girl or boy

Excitement here for you
True self you can renew
Not easy being who you are
Only way to carry far

No to mundane diversions
Gifts deserve their excursions
Follow purity holy ways
Burn off chaff with laser gaze

Leave the haze to survive
Engage air where you thrive
Get quiet still to your core
Voices say what you're here for

Have you experienced the bliss of being and doing what you came here for?
What do you need to change to stay connected?

6 CELEBRATING

Imagine now here in this place
Dancing a goal of the human race
Experiment godhead had in mind
Aim toward joy what a find

Engaged always in a rush
So serious taking on too much
Experience a hardened edge
In transactions create a wedge

Including how we deal with self
Put intensity back on the shelf
End of days leave your body
While here don't miss the party

Discover what makes you high
Communion not head in the sky
Remember get what you give
Don't sit alone engage live

Who are you with on this journey
Not Nobel's PhD's piles of money
In life ask am I celebrating
Joy you feel the best calibrating

What celebrating brings you joy?
Will you experience and schedule it?

7 SOARING

Support accept honor thou
Other is primary tomorrow now
Best for them your inspiration
Presence generates motivation

Fulfilling caring for other
Losing self to sacred mother
It is not about getting
Let go to serving never fretting

Trust encircles life you live
Fill your heart joyously give
Meaning from deep caring
Foundation enables that daring

When tired lonely low
Remember others fill you so
Focus on them fills your being
Third-body enables seeing

R
efreshed go forward again
Blessings strengthen you then
New heights of soaring delight
Carry you very far each night

Who benefits from nurturing and how can you support them in their grail?
What gifts of your giving have you experienced?

8 TIME

Focused linear precise defined
How we hold framed in mind
Known dimension count each day
Defines rhythms structures a way

When young passed slowly
Older each second holy
Closer we get to end of daze
Speeds like gravity many ways

At times abundant at times little
Having more I could fiddle
Commodity try to control
Learn to manage even own

Mastering this ethereal thing
Wake-up startles with its ring
At a metaphysical level
All is now in this revel

Now the only real moment in time
Past or future conjecture of mind
Time a context for sorting
That frame think of aborting

Everything in conscious present
It's all now no need regret it
No need waiting envision in dreams
All here now no matter what seems

How does thinking about time impact behavior?
Are there ways of thinking that would be more resourceful?

9 SPARKLING

What a living animated word
Evokes sparklers soaring birds
Childlike happiness Santa glee
Filled with laughter sense of free

Starts with a grin on your face
Smiling wide eyes sharing grace
Expansion animation merry
Presence lights sundae's cherry

Pulsing alive vibration
Regardless of mood excitation
Knowing you're taken care of
No need to search for love

Look back realize it's true
Life takes care whatever you do
Trust decisions they work out
Realization engenders a joyful shout

Comfort sensing god on your side
No need to push OK feeling pride
Sacred essence scrubbed with delight
Glowing sparkling a gift of white light

When last did you experience such joy?
What was the source and what prevents repeating that today?

10 LONGING

Edginess disturbing sleep
Internal sadness so you weep
Longing peace you pray for
Lonely days endless nights galore

What troubles you awake
Robs essence of what's at stake
Noisy dialogue chatters inside
Upsets your magic carpet ride

Where do you go for solace inside
How to return your sense of pride
What of the aching gnawing grind
Craving freedom of your mind

Fear what may become of you
Will what you hold dear slip through
Attraction for your wanted mate
An anchor for your stalwart faith

Where's the rest of your team
The peace in your precious dream
Where to go when feeling punk
The key to unlock your simmering funk

What are you searching for and how will you know your longing is satisfied?
What if there is nothing to find but inner peace?

11 OCEAN

Rolling undulation soft quiet roar
Timeless forever a footstep's door
Reverie lingers in a sweet mist
Whisper of breeze a delightful kiss

Peaceful serenity nurturing womb
Ageless abiding of nature's tomb
Endless journey each moment whole
Place to float easily your drifting soul

Reverent gratitude for sacred bliss
In a world haywire nothing's amiss
Simple profound sense
There is nothing else

No place to go nothing to hide
Let go illusion and foolish pride
Knowing smile precious dimple
Relax in faith of purpose simple

Dance celebrate laugh contemplate
Attract let go let hips gyrate
Deepening easy let go of striving
No fear or worry about surviving

Already written already so
No pretending what you don't know
Anchor footsteps right here in now
Drink in eternity OK you know how

When have you felt the bliss of certainty?
Can you let go and step into that state?

12 NOW

All now no future or past
Time a fantasy illusory swath
What we know housed in mind
Transpiring now sometimes blind

All takes place head of a pin
That fact a permanent grin
You hold all you'll ever know
Clarity resides in your snow

Watch sheep plan save retire
Common dream does not inspire
Truths abides myth's control
Fear based illusions trample soul

Heed warnings follow your heart
Pure presence comes in fits and starts
Live from inside you already know
In present moments honor the glow

Enduring strength in what's for you
Value not in games others do
Follow masses a molasses bath
Answers on your fluid path

How are you influenced by the hopes, dreams, aspirations, values of others?
What would life be if you followed yourself?

13 PAIN

Different flavors and intensity
Some a little some suffer immensely
Primal scream in solar plexus
Scorched brain seeking nexus

Profound anguish at the core
In body get what we came for
In pure spirit liberated free
Here vehicle demands constantly

No darting here there
Handmaiden space time fear
Subject to corporeal pain
Injury disease stresses strain

Body addicted to people things
Can't let go of longing it seems
One day wake up feel letting go
No longer gripping holding so

From precious letting go of fear
Discover pain not very real
Transcend thoughts that entwine
Heading home there in no time

Do you know suffering is optional?
If discontinued and no longer available, how would you fill time and space?

14 GIFTING

Focus who owns what
Accumulate often for naught
Doesn't heal sadness or cure ills
Cold alone never warms chills

Think of where life could be
In service and charity
Amusing about Manhattan
$26 of little matter

No sense owning earth
Land a public gift of birth
All we need this bountiful planet
Can we learn to share what's on it

Technology science gifts of invention
Providing all let's harness intention
All have roof food vocation
Joyous place abundant creation

Hold this vision no sacrifice
Remember gifts give twice
What you share back to you
A hospitable planet simple true

Have enough, what's missing?
Are you a giver or taker and what's more satisfying?

15 TRAVELING

Different energy left coast right
Left more ethereal right isn't light
Clarity knows which is home
Without certainty destiny roam

Back forth seek perfect union
Weather's hot feeling confusion
Clarity neither's better
Though one is dry other is wetter

Fooling selves wishing there
Happiness resides inside here
Said maturity opens the heart
Lovely thing both sides smart

Sit back drink to your brim
Enjoy where you are not a whim
Send love letters from many todays
Honor all yesterdays

Savor bounty life serves you
No beating self for what you do
Trust emergence curious inside
Honor travels enjoy the ride

Have a noisy internal conversation about your location?
What's the generative way of looking at choices?

16 GEMUTLICH

Connection superlative force
Holding together never divorce
Carries through fire rain
Offers sunlight even in pain

Sharing essence giving smiles
Listening carefully many miles
Joining laughter bearing fears
Revealing scars allowing tears

Speaking dreams making crazy
Lose connection if we get lazy
Counting years connections span
We began without a plan

Draws others unique attraction
Connection friendship traction
Keeps engaging asking more
Glue makes us secure

Gemutlich present feelings warm
Trust engagement new life born
Body rising out of connection
Gives your soul a new dimension

*Do you thank people in your life you share
this connection with? If they died would you
feel bad you had not expressed gratitude?*

17 COLLABORATION

At times alone we do
Projects uniquely you
Birth ideas coming to light
At times struggle fight

Getting thoughts out and down
Takes resolve sometimes frown
Not for a weak state of self-pity
Let discipline keep you witty

Some collaborate with ease
Dancing simple talk a breeze
No ego invested in mine
Give up credit all the time

Others prefer working alone
Grinding fingers to the bone
Artists with clarity precision
Manifest a pure vision

Take on tasks walk your path
Find helpmates before you crash
Assisting comfort when blue
Keep you seeing what is true

Engage personal missions
Look for guidance with revisions
Creative work about iteration
Other heart minds bring salvation

What has been your preference, working alone or collaborating?
What have you discovered about both?

18 HOLIDAY

Holiday holy day if you'll please recall
Reflect on accomplishments and times you did fall
For many time off others and folks fill their plate
Often we forget why we commemorate

Retailers purpose selling stuff
Ecommerce vendors just as much
Card providers lick lips with glee
Fancy food purveyors happy as can be

Some take care of poor souls
Heartbreak depression threw to shoals
Most never stop or recognize
Hollow holes in place of eyes

How to turn an empty face
Install bounce to a halting gait
Understand why a day is profound
Recognize a sacred sound

Spend time in prayer that quiets you
A holy day provides what's true
Honor sacred let go profane
Celebrate holiness let it remain

Aside from respite do holiday's serve a purpose you take time for?
What do they serve and what value do you take?

19 HOLIDAYS

Colors brighter energy highs
Sense of engagement twinkle in eyes
Magical time lights fires within
Mystical glow better than whim

Reverie settling smiles on faces
Compassion graces human races
Smiling face bright shining beam
Longing inside quiet serene

Seeking subsides arising patience
Filling cups of friends and relations
Why the sad sorrowful fact
Why not giving a permanent act

What is it about this time of year
Clicking heels sending cheer
Spirit emerging quelling fear
Perhaps carry this all year

Generosity engenders delight
New heights night after night
This year conscious holding light
Continue giving feeling right

Lessons learned puffing chest
Feeling good giving your best
Give at work to family and friends
Give selflessly that joy has no ends

What's in the way of giving throughout the year?
What would it cost and what's the return?

20 REMEMBERANCE

Born alone so we die
In aloneness sometimes cry
Life at times a delusion
Battling our inner confusion

Periodically wake in the dream
In our sweet biological machine
Now and then oneness visits
Then we know wholeness in us

Lessons on our pilgrim's path
Remember avoid your own wrath
In a body we get to feel
Emotions of a corporal real

Know unity from where we came
Disjointed on this human plane
That dimension place called home
Not alone just part of whole

Unity quest drives life on earth
No matter noble or genteel birth
Look for the path back to god
Not serious do wink and nod

What do you remember about other worldly experiences?
Do those memories inform and guide your life?

21 GIVING

Honor caring for another
Focused concern sister brother
Listening anticipate needs
Satisfy wants do sweet deeds

Receiving no matter their wound
Human with nourishing food
Offer presence cherish love
Provide kindness be a dove

Some give with ease grace
Others from a different place
Some resist confined in skin
Cannot abandon fear within

If you release get big embrace
Others needs provide new face
No longer your old inner map
Feet tingle bounce even tap

Look around you can sense
Provide gifts like no one else
Fill what's missing give not take
See sweet apples you must bake

Use ingredients in front of you
Sacred recipes create new roux
Ready to leave others observe
You came to give care and serve

Do you scan your environment for other's needs?
What gifts do you receive caring for others?

22 ASCENSION

Greetings with open arms
Seeing your harms and charms
Soul journey of psyche mind
Questing steps let go each bind

Rarely easy traveling this path
One day angels next day wrath
You're the anchor with firm grip
Arise stumble each fall and trip

Think you traversed the last ledge
Now you're on a very steep edge
Paradoxical present tricks each time
Highs lows breadth of climb

Each spiral rung serves a twist
Closer to heaven more you resist
Breathe drink pure water air
Faith guides footsteps until there

You are shepherd you are sheep
Embrace that no longer weep
Where to focus what words fill mind
You choose nasty kind

Realize you are liege
Take action please
Focus on mindful delight
Realize folly of fight and flight

Wisdom observes you coming through
Embrace the god within that's you

Do you recognize the wisdom of your voices and counsel?
Do you follow the questions and advices?

23 QUICKENING

Christmas nears quickening
As we face our reckoning
Have you been naughty nice
Will Santa visit with spice

In the year did you riot
Settle in to the quiet
Complacent while insides baking
Shake things needing shaking

How did you treat those you love
Honor cherish like a dove
Amends with those forsaken
Face yourself awaken

Stay calm sacred time nearing
Let go what you're fearing
What's in the way of taking on
New habits of consciousness born

Heaven here for taking
Do you choose partaking
Let go anger crime illusion
Engage now a new infusion

What reflections in this sacred time?
What promises about changes do you make?

24 CHRISTMAS EVE

Marking the birth of Christ
Day of reflection day of nice
Remembering Christmas past
Choosing what you want to last

Charting a course for the year
Celebrate bring good cheer
Mask of sadness sent away
Engage commune this sacred day

Acknowledge gifts that are whole
Bless hold cherish be a grateful soul
Let beauty go forth glow and shine
Honor expectations of sacred time

Joy of community touches your being
Love inside impacts your seeing
Listen to your deepest voice
Share next steps rise rejoice

Next year's path unfolds with shine
Time for taking yours and mine
Honor voices follow your heart
Honor spirit as a noble art

Jesus said god is within
Let deity fill you to the brim
Let abundance guide your turnings
Let wisdom manifest all yearnings

Can you take sacred time, forgive and cleanse for the coming year?
How can you fill souls on Christmas?

25 CHRISTMAS

Today is Christmas day of Christ
Day of solace time to think twice
Stores were crowded bustle glow
People excited moving flow

Family spirit moving in all
Joy blessings trips to the mall
Kindness fills us with pleasure light
Day is delightful quenches appetite

Stockings filled earth in good cheer
Can blessings shared last the year
Window for all to look through
What does soul say is time to renew

Now we stand alive and well
Christmas joys inside us swell
Not only lucky fortunate enough
Resides in all no matter how gruff

Encountering souls on your path
Reach inside make sure you laugh
Today is Christmas celebrate Christ
Day of consoling day of nice

Do you honor the contributions of others at Christmas?
How do you get by giving?
What are your favorite Christmas memories?

26 JOY

Glowing warm fullness rich toothy smiles
Deep resonant laughter with you for miles
White teeth paraded lips parted wide
Whatever the rift gone the divide

Hands touching others grins ear to ear
Flaming hearts speaking voices with cheer
Profound sense of wellness having arrived
Now is the time for you to thrive

Here this moment destiny calls
This precious instant joy bounces off walls
Starts in the cavernous center of soul
Vibration expanding fills up the whole

Overflowing goodness sparkling with light
Energetic abundance lifts you in flight
Fueling action from deep in your core
Hard to imagine you want any more

Emboldened presence encircling you
Results of stewing the recipe that's you
Get what you're giving it all comes back
So keep on flowing riding your track

What is joy, where does it come from, and how do you express, empower and share it?
What value does it have for you and community?

27 DECEMBER

Blustery cold wind chill ice
Venturing outside not very nice
Days squeezing shorter freezing nights
Wet snow falling must shovel twice

Old year ending frayed at its seams
Christmas completed with pregnant dreams
Pretense celebrating smiles false and worn
Way too much hopping from store to store

For some time with blessed family around
Others lonely blank eyes staring down
Reflection deepens looking inside
Gaze at year's journey what's left behind

Resolutions for what's wanted next
Set goals visions along with new tests
If you are lucky smart awake
Get to thank friends for gifts of grace

Remember brandy and glowing hot embers
Filling your insides so many remembers
Looking forward to a coming year
Acknowledge the servers providing good cheer

How do you learn from year end reflection?
What you can do differently this coming year?

28 DECISIONS

Wasteful sitting on fences
Can't depend on anyone else's
Turn left turn right
Stay put in fright

Good bad plus minus ledger
Evaluate next endeavor
Meditate pray divine intervention
Flip a coin Franklin close clarify intention

Beat yourself love yourself ignore indecision
Go to bed let your head indulge in revision
Fool yourself someone else think you are stronger
When time draw the line dawdle no longer

Sink or swim vote is in new ground before you
Win or lose you must choose or it's done for you
Here you are passed the bar of your indecision
Now the truth no super sleuth could do your revision

Another thought rarely taught profound in its meaning
Struggles that have you gripped never leave you beaming
So choose quick make a pick no extensive cogitation
Down the road it unfolds from your revelation

As you sit all these words stifle your intention
Truth be known at the bone no matter direction
Good and bad in every choice each decision fruitful
Just declare you are there deciding is so useful

Do you realize there might not be any such thing as
a right decision? Do you know you can choose again?

29 BESTWORK

Keeps you focused easy to do
Engages mind body spirit too
About identity self-discovery
Finding out who you can't help be

Place of learning to discover
Understand stories with another
A joyful escape
A place to be great

Provides traction a grounding force
A compelling sacred source
Think who you could be
Get serious about legacy

Clear on mission make a plan
Gather intentions expand wingspan
Scale down be earnest get to work
One foot then next discover worth

Let others see no hiding or shrinking
Stay on path not too much blinking
As time is shorter for measuring self
BestWork engages everyone else

Do you have a personal mission expressing the purpose you're here for?
Have you been living and working with that in mind?

30 GRACE

Serenely quiet chattering mind
Illusion unveiled no longer blind
Peaceful presence visits home
Here to forever never alone

Did guides reveal your path
While navigating bliss and wrath
Vision undaunting challenged stretched
Sometimes joyful sometimes wretched

All forgiven trespasses allowed
Let go of anger and proud
Was never you turning dials
A plan had you log many miles

Arrived at this graceful place
To do with pains to erase
Look at the journey what you learned
Now mentor others with gifts earned

Learn from teaching what you know
Honor lessons that helped you grow
Let that presence blanket the land
Embrace wisdom understand

Carry water chop wood on the road
Acknowledge honor the heavy load
Never more than you could hold
No complaints as voices told

Only way out is through
Don't give up traveling keep moving through
The gift of effort a contented soul
Solace of learning you were always whole

What make you feel blessed?
Do you count blessings and acknowledge their presence?

31 TRANSITION

Periodically off yourself
You became someone else
Actions reveal deeper sense of being
Observe from a new place of seeing

Surroundings may imprison a soul
Wherever you turn not feeling whole
Rearrange shed too tight skin
Repot yourself redefine your win

Leave people places behind
Cross rivers let go old binds
Find wisdom within without
Time for sages let go self-doubt

Shed old self good-bye leave behind
Walk alone so you can find
Align with who you might become
Self-supported you feel as one

Sadness aloneness emptiness too
Concern what will become of you
Begin new life you have no choice
Enjoy awake take time rejoice

Notice habitual ways of thinking and being?
What fosters newness and helps transitions?

ABOUT STEWART LEVINE

Stewart Levine is a Resolutionary

S tewart is a creative problem solver widely recognized for creating agree-
ment and empowerment in the most challenging circumstances. He
improves productivity while saving the enormous cost of conflict. His inno-
vative work with "Agreements for Results" and his "Resolutionary" conver-
sational models are unique. As a practicing lawyer he realized that fighting
was a very ineffective way of resolving problems. As a marketing executive
for AT&T he saw that the reason collaborations fall apart is thatpeople do
not spend the time at the beginning of new working relationships to create
clarity about what they want to accomplish together, and how they will get
there. This is true for employment relationships, teams, joint ventures and
all members of any virtual team. As a result of his observations he designed
conversational models that create "Agreements for Results," and a quick
return to productivity when those working relationships break down. He
uses his approach to form teams and joint ventures in a variety of situations.
He works with individuals, couples, partners, small and large organizations
of all kinds. "His models for problem solving, collaboration and conflict
resolution were endorsed by the house judiciary committee."

Among many others he has worked for 3M; American Express; Chevron; Con-Agra; EDS; General Motors; Oracle; Safeco; University of San Francisco; U.S. Departments of Agriculture and the Navy. His "Cycle of Resolution" was selected for inclusion in the "Change Handbook, 3d Edition. *Getting to Resolution: Turning Conflict into Collaboration* (Berrett-Koehler 1998) (Second Edition Oct. 2009) was an Executive Book Club Selection; Featured by Executive Book Summaries; named one of the 30 Best Business Books of 1998 and called "a marvelous book" by Dr. Stephen Covey. It has been translated into Russian, Hebrew and Portuguese. *The Book of Agreement* (Berrett-Koehler 2003) has been endorsed by manythought leaders. It has been hailed as "more practical" than the classic *Getting to Yes* and named one of the best books of 2003 by CEO Refresher (www.Refresher.com). He co-authored *Collaboration 2.0: Technology and Tools for Collaboration in a Web 2.0 World* (Happy About 2008) provides guidance for effectively communicating in the virtual world. Stewart curated and edited *The Best Lawyer You Can Be: Guide to Physical, Mental, Emotional and Spiritual Wellness* for the American Bar Association.

Stewart teaches communication, conflict management and Emotional Intelligence for ResolutionWorks, The American Management Association and The Consulting Team. He has been a lecturer at the University of California Berkeley Law School and the MBA program at Dominican University of California. Stewart was inducted into the College of Law Practice Management.

He is available for Poetry Readings, Personal Coaching, Consulting, Mediation and Relationship and Organizational Interventions. You can reach him through his website http://www.StewartLLevine.com; his email ResolutionWorks@msn.com or his mobile 510-814-1010.